WEST VANCOUVER MEMORIAL LIBRARY

Barcode on front

1168

I0646506

REFERENCE USE ONLY

WEST VANCOUVER MEMORIAL LIBRARY

Withdrawn from Collection

Williams
10178 9.50
4/83

WEST VANCOUVER MEMORIAL LIBRARY

Collecting Decanters

JANE HOLLINGWORTH

MAYFLOWER BOOKS · NEW YORK

CHRISTIE'S INTERNATIONAL COLLECTORS SERIES

To Trude, Eric and Marion
in gratitude for a long and lasting friendship

In the same series:

Fans (Susan Mayor)

Microscopes (Gerard L'Estrange Turner)

Original Prints (Rosemary Simmons)

Phonographs and Gramophones (Christopher Proudfoot)

Victorian Ceramic Tiles (Julian Barnard)

Forthcoming books in the same series:

Decorative Lamps 1890–1930 (Albrecht Bangert)

Frontispiece: A fine early blue Venetian bottle flask in dark blue glass enamelled in iron red, yellow, blue, ochre, white and dark brown from the last quarter of the fifteenth century. (Christie's).

All rights reserved under International and Pan American Copyright Convention. Published in the United States by Mayflower Books, Inc., 575 Lexington Avenue, New York City 10022. Originally published in England by Studio Vista, a division of Cassell Ltd., 35 Red Lion Square, London WCIR 4SG

No part of this publication may be reproduced, stored in a retrieval system, or transmitted, in any form or by any means, without prior written permission of the publishers. Inquiries should be addressed to Mayflower Books, Inc.

Library of Congress Cataloging in Publication Data
Hollingworth, Jane, 1944–
Collecting Decanters

(Christie's international collectors series)
  Bibliography: p.
  1. Decanters – Collectors and collecting.
I. Title. II. Series.
NK5440. D4H64   748.8′2   80-10706

ISBN: 0 8317 2161 8

Manufactured in Hong Kong

First American edition 1980

Contents

REFERENCE USE ONLY
WEST VANCOUVER MEMORIAL LIBRARY

Introduction

When glass is first drawn from the crucible in its molten state, it forms into a perfect globular or tear shape at the end of the blow-rod. This is the basis of all decanter shapes. The expertise of the chemist and the technician goes into the colour, the texture and the light-refracting qualities of the metal; the eye and the skill of the craftsman-blower go into the perfecting of the decanter's final shape; and the imagination of the artist goes into the painted, engraved or cut decoration which further adorns it. Even when made by the same craftsman and decorated by the same hand there will always be subtle differences between individual free-blown decanters. Each piece is unique. It is exactly this originality which keeps the collector for ever on the trail of new and better examples.

When it comes to the various types of decanter the range is enormous, and truly international. Throughout its history the decanter has been afforded the full range of decorative treatment, with countries seeming to take it in turns to perfect a particular style or technique. In Medieval times the market was dominated by the Venetians who first became expert in applied decoration. Then the Germans and Bohemians began to excel in engraved work, the Dutch gained an international reputation for stippled motifs, while the English and Irish were soon acknowledged masters of glass-cutting. Then, in the late nineteenth century, the French emerged as leaders of the new Art Nouveau style, quickly emulated by the Americans, and the English blossomed into artistic engraving of the highest quality. On into the twentieth century and in recent years the Swedish and Scandinavian artists have come to the fore along with their modern Italian counterparts who have re-established Venice as an important centre for new and exciting forms of decorative glass.

Throughout its long history the trade in glass has been as international as the trade in porcelain. At the courts of Henry VIII and Elizabeth I, for example, pride of place was given to the fine examples of Venetian glass whose value was equal to similar items of silver or gold. Yet only a few hundred years later it was the English and Irish cut-glass which was to be the most sought-after in Europe. In salerooms throughout Europe and America locally-made decanters rub shoulders with their imported brothers and sisters. This book is an attempt to illustrate the vast variety of decanters available to the collector, while at the same time providing collectors with sufficient information to be able to identify the possible country of origin and to date the many different decanters which they are likely to encounter.

1 An English Art Nouveau bottle-decanter in green glass depicting an enamelled gothic-style portrait of a young girl. It was executed by Nelia Casella and dated 1892.

7

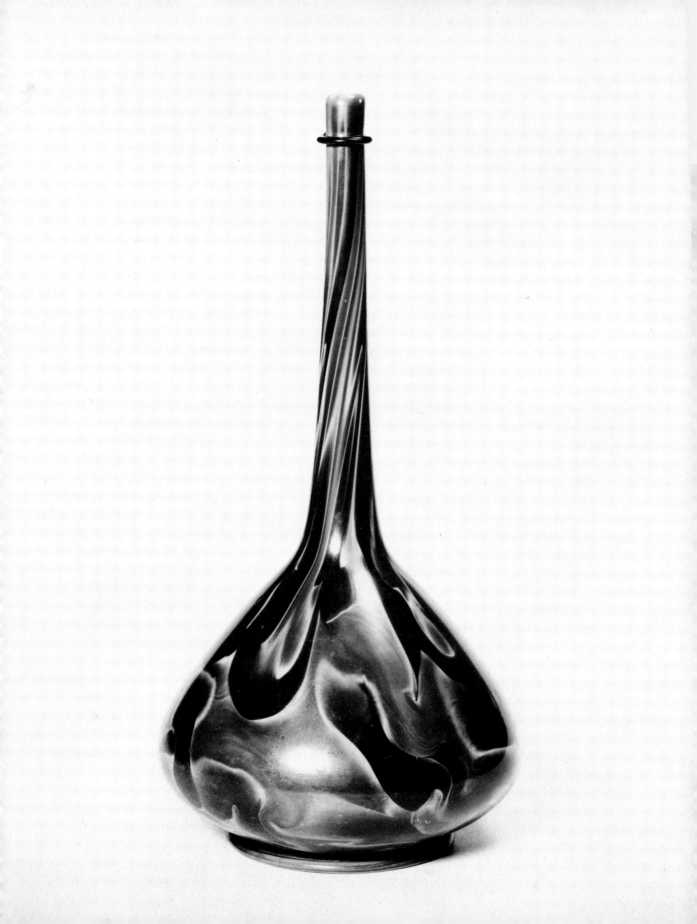

1

The History of Glass-making

It is generally assumed that the secret of glass-making was first discovered somewhere in Asia Minor, Syria, or Egypt, around six thousand years ago. The discovery was probably made by pure accident, for the basic constituents of glass, silica (pure fine sand), together with either soda (marine plants), or potash (basic woodash) would have been readily found within the Middle Eastern environment. All that would have been needed would have been the application of sufficient heat to fuse the components into a new metal – glass.

We know today that, depending on the proportions in which these primitive ingredients were mixed, a wide variety of metals could have been produced. At one extreme, if too much silica was added, the resultant hard, transparent glass would have been soluble in water. If too little silica was present, then the glass would have been too viscous, in the molten state, to be pulled or shaped. Obviously in this dawn of glass-making history only trial and error would have produced a consistent form of glass.

Egyptian glass

It was the Egyptians, closely followed by the Syrians, who successfully carried out the early experiments. Initially, they dealt only with the cooled metal, using it, very much in the manner of stone, as a decorative substitute for precious and semi-precious stones in the making of jewellery, the earliest examples extant being a collec-

tion of glass beads and amulets dating back to around 4000 B.C. which are now in the Egyptian Museum, Cairo.

Gradually, however, they began to explore the possibilities of manipulating glass in its molten state. By the twentieth century B.C. they were able to make hollow glass vessels by creating a sand-core of the desired shape, wrapping it in linen and then dipping the core into molten glass. Once the glass had cooled, the core could be removed, and the vessel was ready for use.

As the Egyptians became more expert at the process so their glasswares became more colourful and more decorative. They found that by kneading and pulling the molten glass, while still on the core, they could fashion spouts, lips and feet. As an alternative to making vessels of only one colour glass, strands of glass in contrasting colours could be wrapped round the core and then gently pulled to achieve a wide variety of multi-coloured wave-like patterns. Mosaic, marbles and mottled effects could be obtained by sticking chunks of cooled coloured glass to the core and then refiring. Using techniques such as these they were able to imitate a comprehensive range of semi-precious stones from agates to bloodstones.

2 An imitation in glass of semi-precious stone. This Venetian flask of c. 1500, like the later bottle decanter, is an attempt to mimic agate (calcedonio). Height 14¾ in. (Victoria and Albert Museum).

However there were two significant gaps in the Egyptian knowledge of glass technology. In the first instance, they had never discovered the secret of how to make really clear colourless glass, and in the second instance they had failed to conceive the idea of blowing glass to make hollow vessels, rather than making them of core-glass. Both these major discoveries belong to the period of the Roman Empire.

Roman glass

Of the two it was the art of glass-blowing which was discovered first; most probably in Sidon, in Syria, about a century before the birth of Christ. Prior to its discovery, objects made of glass had tended to be small — bottles for oil, scent and the like; small jugs and amphoras. With the arrival of blowing techniques, much larger vessels of thinner glass could be attempted.

Within two or three years, the invention of colourless glass followed. In our modern world, where the majority of everyday glassware is colourless, it comes as a surprise to learn that it took several thousand years of coloured glass production before man came up with the discovery of a true colourless glass. The root of the problem lay in the components of the *batch*, or mixture of ingredients, from which the glass was made. In their natural state all are found together with impurities, especially iron, which, though present in even minute quantities, leaves the glass with a decidedly greenish tinge.

3 A Roman jug dating from the second century A.D. The shape of this jug foreshadows that of the early bottle-decanters of fourteen hundred years later. (Victoria and Albert Museum).

4 Examples of early third- and fourth-century Roman glass showing shapes which were popular for the next 1600 years and led to the iridescent movement of the nineteenth century. (Victoria and Albert Museum).

The Roman solution to the problem, according to Pliny, was the addition to the batch of minute quantities of *magnes lapis*, by which he probably meant manganese. It was an extremely delicate process in which the amount of decolourizing agent had to exactly balance the amount of impurities present. Too little decolourizer and the greenish tinge remained; too much decolourizer and the glass turned a pinkish colour.

Fast on the heels of colourless glass, came advances in methods of decorating it. It is true that the Egyptians had been the first to apply the cutting wheel to glass; but the Romans should be credited with being the first to fully explore its potential. Initially, clear glasswares were shallow cut with faceted geometric patterns to enhance the basic brilliance of the metal, then, gradually pictorial cutting and engraving were developed, so that by the fourth century AD the first commemorative glassware had been produced, depicting the arena struggles of athletes, gladiators and charioteers, the names of the participants appearing beneath the picture of the event. From these early experiments in glass-cutting evolved the art of cutting cased glass in cameo relief, a more detailed discussion of which comes in Chapter 5.

The rise of Islamic glass

As the Roman Empire spread, so too did the full vocabulary of Roman glass-technology. New glass-centres were soon established throughout the length and breadth of Europe and across the Channel in Britain. The Roman craftsmen who established these new centres were well-versed in the arts of gilding, enamelling, and painting, as well as cutting and engraving. When the Empire collapsed, however, it was not only the Roman troops who pulled out of the occupied territories. With them went the Roman glass-makers and the knowledge which they had brought with

5 Early mould blown glass. The body of this honey-coloured ewer was made in Persia in the twelfth and thirteenth-century period by blowing it into a dimpled mould. (Victoria and Albert Museum).

them. Supplies of raw materials which had been transported so efficiently from one end of the Empire to the other were no longer available. The manufacture of glass, while still carried out in Northern Europe, became a pitiful affair compared to earlier production at the height of the Empire. With the Roman Empire in ruins it was the

6 *Early attempts to break with Venice: A French flask of semi-opaque blue glass with a central portrait medallion; c 1550. Height 12½ ins. (Victoria and Albert Museum).*

tion. With the Fall of Damascus in 1402 the intitiative in glass-making passed back to Europe.

Venetian glass

The city poised and ready to take over the role of major glass-producer was Venice. Glass-making had been established in the city since 450 AD when glassworkers fled there from the Adriatic port of Aquileia which was being overrun by Attila the Hun. Venice was an ideal position from which to operate. Essential materials could be shipped in from all over the known world, but perhaps of much greater importance was the fact that knowledge of glass techniques could easily be exchanged with traders from other parts of the Mediterranean, especially those from the Islamic world.

By the thirteenth century, glass-making in Venice was thriving to such an extent that the numerous glass-houses had become a fire-hazard to the city and the decision was made to move both glass-houses and workers to the nearby island of Murano. Decorative glass, however, proved to be such a source of wealth that the glassworkers soon became virtual prisoners on the island. Anyone found betraying information about methods of production faced severe punishment, and even death, at the hands of the law.

The strict controls obviously worked. Despite the fact that a few spirited workers managed to escape from the island to set up in business elsewhere in Europe, Venice held a virtual glass monopoly, within Europe, from the thirteenth century right through to the dawn of the seventeenth century.

Part of the key to their success lay in their early mastery of enamelling and gilding glass which they had learned from their trade with Islam. But they were also innovators in their own right. Their supreme achievement was the evolution of *cristallo*, a transparent, white metal glass,

Islamic world which carried on the tradition of glasswork. Indeed, in the sphere of enamelling it could be argued that Islamic glass far surpassed that of its predecessors. By the tenth century AD they were at the peak of their production, but again it was the political unrest of the period which led to a sudden and dramatic decline in produc-

which was much purer than the Roman *crystallum* of centuries before.

The main components of the batch were white pebbles from the beds of the Rivers Po and Ticino, together with a marine soda-ash from Spain and Egypt. The end result of this fusion was a light, delicate, clear metal which was extremely easy to manipulate in its molten state. It could be applied in thin delicate trails, blobs and threads to the exterior of vessels or used as thin opaque white rods blown in clear glass to form delicate lacy patterns within the glass. The decorative styles which the Murano workers developed was so individual to the Venetians that subsequent imitative glassware produced elsewhere in Europe is termed *'façon de Venise'* glass.

The spread of the knowledge of glass techniques

The handful of men who managed to escape from Murano fled to major cities like London, Paris, and Antwerp, to set up their rival businesses, and they were joined in this dissemination of glass technology by master glass-makers from the town of L'Altare near Genoa who, as early as the ninth century AD had grouped themselves into guilds with the express purpose of spreading their knowledge throughout Europe and establishing new glass-making centres.

Although the knowledge of glass-making spread quite rapidly, the rest of Europe did not have the trading links which enabled the Venetians to import their raw materials from around the Mediterranean. The *barilla*, a marine plant from salt-marshes near Alicante in Spain, together with *roquetta*, another marine plant from Egypt and the Near East, were the essential soda sources for the standard pale-yellow, smoky-grey Venetian glass. In Northern France, England and Scandinavia the new glass-houses found that they could substitute ashes from the locally obtainable kelp

(a type of seaweed) and still retain the Venetian lightness of weight and plasticity. But the inland areas of France and Germany had to find other alternatives.

In France, the solution was the local *verre de fougère* which used potash, made from the ashes of bracken found in the large tracts of forest in areas like Dauphine, instead of soda. In Bohemia and Northern Germany the soda-substitute was potash made from the ashes of beechwood which produced the distinctive *Waldglas* (literally 'forest glass'). In both instances the potash-glass had a much stronger greenish, brownish or yellowish tinge to it, and was a much harder, brilliant metal.

7 *In the absence of high-quality clear glass, the rich made use of vessels like this decanter jug, dating from the sixteenth century, made of rock crystal and mounted in silver-gilt and set with gems. (Victoria and Albert Museum).*

13

The history of early English glass

When the Romans had withdrawn from the province in 410 AD the manufacture of glass in Britain had gradually ground to a halt, and for the next seven hundred years the British were forced to import their glass from well-established continental glass-making areas like those in Normandy, the Rhineland and Lorraine, or Venice.

Exactly how or when the glass-making industry returned, is still shrouded in the mists of history, but it can be presumed that the first glaziers must have come to settle in the wake of the Norman Conquest. Certainly, the records show that by the mid-thirteenth century, glass-making, under the leadership of Laurence Vitrearius of Normandy, was well-established along the wooded belt of the Weald which stretches from west to east across the counties of Sussex, Surrey, and Kent, some twenty miles south of London.

The fact that these foreign glaziers had chosen the Weald in which to settle was no coincidence. Unlike the Venetians who used soda-ash as the alkali in their batch, the Seine-Rhine tradition, brought over by Vitrearius, made use of wood-ash and similar vegetable matter as a fluxing material. Because of this, kilns had to be established in forested areas where there were sufficient supplies of both wood and vegetation for fuel and materials.

The bulk of this early production was inevitably stained glass for the windows of the ecclesiastical building projects. Domestic glassware took a definite second place in the form of a wide variety of household items from lamps to bottles, cups, beakers, and phials all made from heavy potash-glass. But gradually the artistic side of production began to emerge, and finally dominate.

As England became more affluent, so glass-ware began to appear not only on the tables of the royal palaces but in the dining halls of the nobility up and down the land. Rivalry between England and Venice was bitter. All depended on whether or not the monarchy was prepared to restrict the import of Venetian wares. Richard II, for example, must have dealt the local industry a cruel blow when, in 1399, he granted permission to a couple of Venetian ships to sell their glass in the port of London, free of any duties.

Queen Elizabeth I, on the other hand, had a more protective attitude. Under her *aegis* a continental merchant by the name of Jean Carré, was allowed to introduce several families of glass-makers from Antwerp and Lorraine into the Weald area to breathe new life into the industry. The project was successful and by the time of his death he had set up a glasshouse in London itself. It is probable that the established glass-makers in the Weald must have resented the intrusion of these foreigners, for, soon after Carré's death, the new-comers moved their operations away from the Weald to fresh sites in Hampshire, Gloucestershire, and the West Country.

But the seeds of a revitalized glass industry had been sown by Carré in the shape of his Crutched Friars glasshouse in London. This was taken over, on Carré's death in 1572, by Giacomo Verzelini, a Venetian who arrived in England after spending several years in the Antwerp glass industry. He managed to persuade the Queen to grant him a special twenty-one-year licence 'for the makyne of drinkynge glasses suche as be accustomablie made in the towne of Murano' on the understanding that he would pass on this knowledge to the English glass-makers, and, most important of all, that all import of foreign glass would be banned.

All went well until 1615, the year in which Elizabeth's successor, James I, issued his 'Proclamation Touching Glasses'. For the past two or three hundred years the forests of England had been disappearing at an alarming rate as more and more trees were chopped down for use in the building of ships and houses. King James called a halt to it. His proclamation forbade the use of wood as a fuel for glass-making.

8 The skill of the Venetian craftsmen. Right: a ewer in coloured millefiori. Left: the rich glow of adventurine. (Victoria and Albert Museum).

9 Throughout the sixteenth and seventeenth century Venice still dominated the European market. A combination of talents: this ewer had a body of Venetian latticino glass, but the silver mounts bear early seventeenth-century Nuremberg hall marks.

Seventeenth-century developments in England

The man who saved the English industry was Sir Robert Mansell, a retired Admiral who had, as his sole qualifications for the task, a sound head for business. Of the actual technicalities of glass-making he knew nothing, but he was quick to learn. If they could not use wood, then let them use coal. Under his directions the glass-making industry was reorganized on a national scale, with mines for sea-coal and pit-coal established throughout the country. The kilns had to be re-developed, new pots had to be designed, the whole emphasis of glass-making shifted. No longer tied to being close to wood fuel, new centres sprang up near the coalfields and expanded in places like Stourbridge, Newcastle-on-Tyne, Swansea, the Trent Valley, and Kings Lynn. From Wemyss in Fife to Newham-on-Severn, London, and Purbeck Island, Mansell had the sole patent from James I for the making of glass 'of any fashion, stuff, matter or metal whatsoever with sea cole, pitt coale or any other fewell whatsoever not being tymber or wood'. Under his influence too, the glaziers themselves became organized into the Glass Sellers' Company which was given its first royal Charter by Charles I in 1635.

All was set for an era of success and expansion in the industry such as had never been seen before. Then political disaster struck. The Civil War broke out and it was not until the monarchy was restored in 1660, when Bonnie Prince Charlie returned to London to be crowned Charles II, that peace came once again to the country. As the famous diarist, John Evelyn, wrote, that entry into London by the king was a triumphant one with 'above 20,000 horse and foote, brandishing their swords and shouting with inexpressable joy; the wayes strew'd with flowers, the bells ringing, the streets hung with tapissry, fountains running with wine . . . I stood in the Strand and beheld it, and bless'd God.'

The glass-makers also had reason to bless God for Charles' return, for in 1664 he reconstituted the Charter of the Glass Sellers' Company. The stage was therefore set for a dramatic revival of the industry. The affluent restoration society was extravagant with its spending, and hot in pursuit of luxury. The Glass Sellers were there with the sole object of satisfying these needs. Theirs was a dual role. On the one hand they had a thriving business importing Venetian glass, and on the other they did what they could to encourage and foster the growth of the English home industry. This ambiguity of interests must have disheartened the English glass-makers to a certain extent, especially in view of the large quantities of Venetian glass being imported . . . one London firm of John Greene and Michael Measey for example, imported no less than two thousand dozen glasses and over one thousand looking-glass plates in the five-year period between 1667 and 1672.

What eventually swung the pendulum in favour of the English industry, however, was the fact that the Venetians were beginning to pay less and less attention to the quality of the glass which they sent over.

George Ravenscroft

As far as the Glass Sellers were concerned there was only one solution to the problem: the English industry had to be brought up to the Venetian standard. With this end in view they appointed George Ravenscroft to review the English glass industry. Ravenscroft was an excellent choice. A wealthy shipowner whose vessels plied the Mediterranean trading between England and countries like Turkey and Italy, he had plenty of time to indulge in his favourite hobby of chemistry. As the bulk of his cargo from Venice was glass-ware, it was the chemical make-up of glass which came to intrigue him more and more. In 1612, an Italian, Antonio Neri, had published one of the first really authoritative works on glass-making

entitled *L'Arte Vetraria* which described, in considerable detail, the formulae, methods, and means of producing glass. In 1662, Christopher Merret, a member of the newly formed Royal Society of London, translated the work into English under the title of *The Art of Glass*, and there is little doubt that when Ravenscroft first began his research in the early 1670s, he would have had ready access to the book. By 1673, the Sellers had installed Ravenscroft in a new glass-house in the Savoy, with an Italian workman by the name of Da Costa as assistant. After only eight months' work, Ravenscroft came up with a new glass, which promised to be an excellent substitute for Venetian crystal.

The name which Ravenscroft chose for his new glass was *fflint crystalline*. It was a true marriage between the Venetian and the traditionally English formulae. As in the *Waldglas*, potash was used as the basic alkali flux, but the new innovation was the use in the batch of transparent English flints. All augured well. The Savoy house began production of the new glass-ware, made to the designs and specifications laid out by the Glass Sellers' Company.

However, although not apparent when the glass left the Savoy premises, after a while a serious defect appeared – the glass 'crisselled', that is, it gradually devitrified and became a clouded mass of tiny hair-line faults which rendered vessels virtually opaque in the more extreme cases. 'Flint crystalline' had to be withdrawn from the market and Ravenscroft began his experiments again.

The new glass of lead

The solution was found by the following year. It was discovered that the crisselling had been due to an excessive amount of potash and that, by substituting either red lead or litharge, an oxide of lead, for a proportion of the potash all further danger

of devitrification was avoided. The Glass Sellers were quick to publicly assure customers that 'the deffect of the flint glasses (which were formerly observed to crissel and decay) hath been redressed . . . and the glasses since made have proved durable and lasting as any glasses whatsoever'. To ensure that buyers did not confuse the flint glass with the latest *glass-of-lead* Ravenscroft was allowed to stamp his own mark, the head of a raven, on all the new-formula glass-ware.

The attributes of the new glass-of-lead were many. It had much greater light-refracting qualities which gave it an almost luminous quality. Its brilliance and fire made the Venetian glass seem dull in comparison. After hundreds of years of searching, this at last, was the nearest that clear glass had come to pure rock crystal. From the point of view of wear and tear, the lead content made the glass-of-lead wares much heavier, and as a result it was far more durable than the fragile Venetian glass. Finally, from the makers' point of view, although it cooled more quickly and therefore only leant itself to stockier heavier shapes, when cut, the light-refracting qualities of the glass burst into such brilliances that for the first time glass-ware could actually surpass rock crystal. The new glass was unquestionably the best in Europe, and the British glass industry began to boom. London still set the tone when it came to style, but already by the end of the century flint glass was being produced at places as far afield as Newcastle-upon-Tyne, the Isle of Wight and Bristol. By 1696, Stourbridge, with no fewer than five glass-houses, was already beginning to challenge the supremacy of London which boasted only nine.

10 A small decanter jug c. 1685. Height 5¹/₈ in.

11 Opposite: Decanter and wine glass from a service by Baccarat, both bearing a medallion with a coat of arms set into the thickness of the wall. French, nineteenth century. (London Museum).

The Glass Excise Act 1745

As will be seen later, in Chapter 6, there was no real knowledge of cutting in Britain before the Treaty of Utrecht in 1713 which allowed German and Bohemian engravers

12 This imitation of a classical English shape was engraved in Germany with the arms of Caroline Felicité of Nassau-Usingen in the 1740s. (Victoria and Albert Museum).

to put their knowledge on the international market, moving freely from one country to another, wherever the work was most lucrative. Experimenting first with engraved decoration, the English were just about to exploit the cut potential of lead glass when the Glass Excise Act of 1745 was imposed in an effort to raise money to finance the various wars which England was caught up in at the time. The tax was levied at the rate of 1d per pound of raw materials, but the ground-up broken glass, known in the business as cullet, which could make up as much as half the weight of the weight of the batch, was not taxed at all.

Obviously, the 1745 Act encouraged a much greater economy of materials but it is dubious whether the customer really felt the presence of the tax at all, for recent technological advances had lead to glass being blown more thinly, so that two vessels could now easily be made for the price of one. The only real difference it made was on the evolution of cut glass. This was checked from becoming too elaborate as soon as it was started because a much thicker glass was needed on which to cut deep facets. Instead the emphasis in England for the rest of the century, was on shallow cuts, like flutes and hollows, or painting, enamelling and engraving techniques which could easily be executed on the thinner vessels.

European developments

This new light-weight crystal glass became the envy of Europe, and the elegant English decanter-shape which was very much at the forefront of the new rococo taste was widely imitated abroad. The eighteenth century saw the sudden growth of many new glass-houses, often under direct royal patronage. The St Petersburg Imperial Glass Factory, established in what is now Leningrad by Tsar Peter I; the Verrerie Royale de Saint-Louis and the Baccarat Glass Factory established in Lorraine under Louis XV; the Royal Glass Works at

La Granja de San Ildefonso near Segovia in Spain under the patronage of Queen Isabella; the Royal Dutch Glass Works at Leerdam, near Utrecht and the Nöstetangen factory near Drammen. Norway, under the patronage of King Christian VI; all these new glasshouses had sprung up independently by the mid-eighteenth century.

Expert glass-makers were much in demand throughout Europe and even in America. The newly-opened Nöstetangen works in Norway induced James Keith and his assistant William Brown to join them from Newcastle-upon-Tyne in 1755; in 1754 a master Swedish glass-maker, Joseph Eder, began work at the Spanish San Ildefonso works; Caspar Wistar, in America, employed four Belgian craftsmen at his New Jersey works; and so the list goes on. The English decanter shapes were widely pirated as too were the German and Bohemian forms of cut, engraved and enamel decoration.

Anglo-Irish cut glass

The popularity of the Bohemian look, however, was about to be overshadowed by the sudden and dramatic rebirth of cut-glass in Britain. The revival was due to two factors. In 1777, the Glass Tax was doubled to raise money to finance the struggle for dominance in the colonies. This Act, like the one before it in 1745 did not apply to Ireland, but that was of little help to the Irish glass-makers as they were forbidden to export their wares. When, however, the Irish export ban was lifted, by Act of Parliament in 1780, the door to expansion was suddenly wide open: no glass tax coupled with freedom to trade on the world market. Seemingly overnight there was a mass exodus of workers from England to people the new glass-houses which had begun to mushroom up in Ireland. With no tax payable on the weight of glass used it was not long before the makers realized that there

was nothing to stop them blowing decanters of much thicker body and decorating them with deep facet-cutting. The development of the industry is dealt with in much greater detail in Chapter 6, here there is only room to point out that cut-glass in the Anglo-Irish style became the most sought-after glassware in Europe until about 1820, and was widely copied in Europe most notably by the Baccarat factory in the west and the St Petersburg factory to the east.

The Irish were fortunate in having their restrictions lifted. In the colonies, however, equally strict controls remained in force. There was an absolute ban on anyone setting up their own manufacturing industries of any kind. The dependency of the Americans on wares imported from the mother country ensured the continuation of a highly profitable and expanding market for the British manufacturers.

The American industry

One of the first men in America to successfully revolt against these restrictions was Caspar Wistar who landed in Philadelphia in 1717 and soon became the owner of a thriving business making brass buttons. It was probably the profits accumulated from this venture which provided the capital for building his glass-house at Allowaystown, southern New Jersey, in 1739. Knowledge of how to make glass came from four Belgian glass-makers who were tempted to America by Wistar's promise that they would be assured of one third of the total profits of the business (plus house, land, food and servants) providing that they swore never to reveal the art of glassmaking to anyone but Wistar and his son. They arrived in New Jersey in 1739 and the glasshouse first opened its doors in 1740. The necessary fuel and sand was to be found in ample supply in the surrounding area, and this, coupled with an increasing reluctance on the part of the colonists to buy imported wares, ensured that Wistar's business was a resounding success. Despite the troubled times it managed to ride through to the early years of the War of Independence and only finally closed down in 1781 when Richard died.

Initially, the output of Wistar's factory was practical: window glass, lamp glasses, retorts, and a whole range of bottles: the sort of everyday glass-ware which the colonists were crying out for. But gradually his products became fancier and more ambitious. As well as clear glass came tinted wares: pale aquamarines, turquoise, amber, emerald, olive green, brown, opaque white: and as the colours on his palette grew in number, so too did the combinations of colours which he would put together in one vessel to create striped patterns similar to the later 'Nailsea' ware in England.

It is presumed that, during the lifetime of Caspar and his son Richard, the workmen at the Wistar factory maintained their vow of secrecy, but when an advertisement appeared in the Pennsylvanian Journal (in 1780) stating that 'the glass manufactory in Salem County, West Jersey, is for sale', one can assume that the Wistar workforce finally considered themselves free to make profitable use of their glass-making expertise as best as they could.

From that first group of Wistar workmen, the knowledge of glass-making spread outwards from Allowaystown like ripples on a pool and gave rise to the style commonly known today among collectors as the 'South Jersey Tradition', which relied heavily on the Venetian tradition of applied and manipulated forms of glass decoration. Where Wistar had succeeded, others soon began to follow. Worth mention in particular is Henry William Stiegel, a native of Cologne, who opened his first glass-house in Elizabeth Furnace in Lancaster County, Pennsylvania, around 1763. He made special visits to Bristol and London to learn about the English glass-making techniques, and then to Europe to master the German and Venetian traditions. So well did his

workforce master the arts of copper-wheel engraving and enamelling that his advertisements were soon able to boast that his glass was 'equal in quality to any imported from Europe'. Unfortunately, his own extravagant tastes led to his bankruptcy in 1774, his glasshouses sold to meet demands from creditors.

A far more modest character was John Frederick Amelung who established the New Bremen Glass Manufactory in Maryland in 1784. Again production was very much in imitation of the popular European wares of the time, but in one particular field Amelung personally excelled – commemorative engraved wares, greater details of which appear later in the book.

Pittsburgh glass

The first Pittsburgh Glass Works in Pennsylvania was started in 1797 by two former Revolutionary Army officers, General O'Hara and Major Craig, and in the same year the New Geneva Glass Works swung into operation in Fayette County founded by Albert Gallatin. It was to factories such as these that some of the Amelung craftsmen must have migrated when the factory finally closed down. With them came the knowledge and expertise which the Pittsburg industries needed.

There were two main advantages which made Pittsburgh an ideal centre for the new thriving glass industry. First, the Colonists had rediscovered the fact that glass furnaces could be fired by coal as well as wood fuel, and Pittsburgh was just beginning to discover how rich it was in coal at a time when timber was running short along the coastal region. Secondly, the further west the frontier was pushed, the more expensive and difficult it became to transport either imported glass or the coastal colonial wares from the sea-board across the Allegheny mountains to central and southern America.

Pittsburgh had begun to stand on its own as

a glass-manufacturing area at just the right time. Not only had the War of Independence improved the roads of America and the riverboats begun to open up river transport, but the later war of 1812, during which the American coast was blockaded, had drastically cut down the amounts of imported glassware and given an added boost to the home industries. Within only a few years of the first glasshouse having been opened, the glass business in and around Pittsburgh was thriving, and by 1826 one of the locals was able to proudly boast, 'The glass of Pittsburgh and the parts adjacent, is known and sold from Maine to New Orleans. Even in Mexico they quaff their beverage from the beautiful white flint of Messrs Bakewell, Page and Bakewell of our city.'

The firm of Messrs Bakewell, Page and Bakewell mentioned in this letter was one of the greatest of the early American glass-houses, and certainly one which produced the most diversified range of products. It was founded in 1807 by two Englishmen, Benjamin Bakewell and Edward Ensell who began producing top quality and engraved glass from the moment it first opened. Such was its success that it soon attracted competition from the east, the strongest contender being the New England Glass Company (N.E.G.C. for abbreviation) of Cambridge, Massachusetts.

Mechanization

So far, in the history of American glass, the main aim of the various glass-manufacturers was to imitate, as closely as possible, the European and Anglo-Irish wares which were being imported into the country in such vast quantities. Gradually, however, the American industry began to go its own way. Demand was so high that more and more makers began to experiment with various methods of short-cutting the lengthy hand-made glass process. The sum total of

13 A typical 'wrythen' decanter bottle, this example in amber glass is probably from the American glassworks at Zanesville, Ohio, c. 1825–1835. (Victoria and Albert Museum).

their efforts was the evolution of pressed and moulded glass, a subject discussed in much greater detail in Chapter 6, suffice it to say here, that so proficient did they become in mass-production, that they effectively killed the British cut-glass market once they had exhibited at the Great Exhibition in 1851.

To quote the *Illustrated Encyclopaedia of the Exhibition*, 'by pressing into moulds this elegant material is produced to the public . . . at prices considerably lower than those at which cut flint glass could be possibly offered. Many of the specimens of pressed glass exhibited have a degree of sharpness in all ornamental parts which renders it difficult, without a close examination, to say whether or not they have been subjected to the glass cutter's wheel.'

It was this that brought an end to the boom in the English cut-glass industry. Only those companies, both in England and America, who could afford to spend their time and energy in creating really first-class high quality cut-glass could survive the next thirty years until the interest in cut glass was renewed. In the meantime, patterned, pressed and moulded glass, like the cuckoo in the nest, tended to push out the other fashionable lines at the lower end of the market.

The Great Exhibition 1851

The Great Exhibition cannot be brushed aside in a single sentence. It was a monumental tribute not only to British industry but to the British glass-makers in particular. It was housed in that vast edifice of glass, the Crystal Palace. The outstanding focal point of the exhibition was a vast twenty-seven foot high cut crystal fountain made by Follet Osler of Birmingham, set right in the centre of the building at the intersection of nave and transept; and, of course, there were numerous British glass manufacturers with their produce on display: seventeen of these were awarded prizes, nine of which were for cut-glass.

The world came to visit, and the world saw, according to one French visitor that 'England has excelled in the manufacture of glass, especially flint glass.' But there was another side to this great fanfare to the achievements of the British industry: other glass manufacturers from all over the world also brought and displayed their wares. Apart from the American pressed and moulded glass, it was the new coloured Bohemian glass which captured the public's imagination, the most eye-catching display being that from the Neuwelt glassworks of Count Harrach. The particular style of glass which he displayed was that in which vessels were blown in one colour of glass and then cased with another layer of coloured glass, the outer surface being cut away in patterns to reveal the differently coloured glass below.

The Bohemian exhibits were the result of continuous experimentation which had been carried out since the 1780s when the Bohemian engravers first felt their markets dwindling in competition with the Anglo-Irish cut glass. If they could not match the brilliance of colourless lead crystal their only alternative was to develop a whole range of beautiful coloured metals. Friedrich Egermann was the glass-maker from northern Bohemia who was at the forefront of the new Bohemian glass. A much more detailed description of his achievements will be found in Chapter 3, but within the context of the overall development of glass in Europe his contribution is formidable. It was the palette, developed by Egermann and his Bohemian contemporaries which contributed further to the decline in English cut-glass. First with flashed glass, decorated with engraving and then with cut, coloured, and opaque-white cased glass, the Bohemians completely dominated the European market, closely followed by the Austrian firm of Lobmeyr in Vienna with their Biedermeier glass.

But technology was gathering momentum so rapidly that the Bohemian wares were soon being avidly copied. As early as 1836

La Société d'Encouragement pour l'Industrie Française had offered prizes for coloured and decorated glass in the Bohemian style, and the French crystalleries were quick to respond. In England, it was round Stourbridge that the new Bohemian look was widely adopted, the technique of casing glass leading directly to the hand-cut 'cameo' glass of John Northwood and his contemporaries. While in America the New England Glass Company, closely followed by the Boston and Sandwich Company, rapidly imitated the Bohemian coloured glass-ware after the American public had shown themselves so impressed by the Austrian exhibits at the 1853 Exhibition in New York's Crystal Palace.

French glass

Up until this second half of the nineteenth century the French had not really made their mark in the realms of decorative glassware. An early specialization in high quality stained glass, much in demand throughout Medieval Europe for the massive ecclesiastical building projects, precluded the Normandy and Lorraine glass-workers from developing an interest in glass for the table. A flourishing crown glass industry then led onto the famous Saint-Gobain works whose mirror-glass was the most sought-after in Europe. From there, with the establishment of Baccarat, St Louis and Clichy, the next speciality took the form of paper-weights. Again France led the rest of Europe in this field. By the late eighteenth century, however, the French factories gradually began to produce decorative tablewares, but it was not until the late nineteenth century that they came dramatically to the fore with the unique Art Nouveau glass of artists like Eugène Rousseau and Gallé. Their subtle use of colour, combined with a whole new range of exciting forms took the glass-making world by storm at the Paris Exhibition of 1878.

14 *Steinschonau hochschnitt: horses on cased or flashed glass. Engraved by Karel Pfohl (1826–1894).*

25

Louis Comfort Tiffany

In Paris at the time (in the process of completing his training as an artist) was Louis Comfort Tiffany, son of a prominent New York jeweller. Through Samuel Bing, he had come into contact with the Art Nouveau movement and it was glass, rather than painting which fired his imagination. On his return to America he opened his first factory in Long Island, New York. Drawing on his experience of the French Art Nouveau glass and marrying it with his own fascination for the iridescence of ancient glass he soon began producing a completely new form or iridescent glass which he termed *'favrile'*. His right-hand man was Arthur J. Nash, a Stourbridge craftsman whose knowledge of glass technology enabled him to put Tiffany's concepts into reality.

The glassware made by these leaders at the forefront of the French and American Art Nouveau movements were individual pieces, hand-made, expensive, and more often than not, signed. The American glass-industry, on the other hand, was geared to mass-production. So it was that companies like the New England Glass Company, under the guiding hand of John Locke, and the more recently formed Steuben Glass Works, under the direction of Frederick Carder, brought out a whole new range of mass-produced coloured 'art glass' in a variety of finishes. In England, the firm of Thomas Webb and Sons were leaders among the many Stourbridge glass-makers who soon took their lead from America. 'Amberina', 'Pomona', 'Peach Bloom', 'Burmese', 'Satin', 'Clutha', 'Ice-glass', 'Adventurine' are but a few of the many new types of glass to pour on to the market from both sides of the Atlantic during the second half of the nineteenth century.

15 Green glass decanter by Gallé decorated with delicate floral motifs for which he was famed.

Italian rebirth

Whereas before the nineteenth century particular styles of glass had lasted for between twenty to fifty years before being eclipsed by a new vogue, in the nineteenth century fashions were of such short a duration that by the end of the century several very different styles were running concurrently. So it was that at the same Paris Exhibition of 1867 glass-makers' attention was also attracted by the work of Antonio Salvati who had returned to the hand-blown Venetian style of form and decoration. This was the beginning of the revival of Murano's international reputation which was sealed in the period from the 1920s onwards by the work of Ercole Barovier, Flavio Poli and Paolo Venini who were to prove the new pioneers of finding new finishes and surface treatments for their coloured glassware.

The new school of engravers

Both the Art Nouveau coloured glass and the Venetian-style hand-blown glass were impressive, but the jury, passing verdicts on the various exhibits at the Paris Exhibition, were unanimously agreed that the 'greatest advance is shown in engraved glass'. By this they did not only mean the *'cameo'* engraving carried out by men like Northwood and Woodall, but the engraving carried out on colourless crystal by men like Frederick Kny and William Fritsche in England and Vaupel, Leighton and Fillebrown at the New England Glass Company in America. Coming nearer to our own time, it was in Sweden that this engraved technique was to reach its height while in America a new brand of studio craftsmen emerged with the development of small kilns which could be easily housed in a one-man studio.

Much more detailed discussions of this diversity of wares from the late nineteenth century onwards will be given in the appropriate specialist chapters which follow.

A brief chronology of glass-making

1240   Laurence Vitrearius, probably from Normandy, established a glasshouse at Dyers Cross, near Chiddingford in Surrey.

From *c* 1300 Venice was exporting glass on a large scale.

1400–1500   By using manganese the Venetians developed *cristallo* a fragile soda glass.

1406   Glassmakers in the Land of Hesse, Germany were well-established.

c 1506   The Colnet family established a glassworks near Mons in Belgium making a *façon de Venise* glass.

1534   The Hall-in-Tyrol glassworks east of Innsbruck was founded in Austria by a German glassworker, Wolfgang Vitl, of Augsburg.

1537   First mention of the Al Gesu glassworks in Murano, run by Antonio Miotti and his descendants from 1542 until the late eighteenth century.

1541   Glassworkers from Murano were recorded in Antwerp (Belgium).

1568   Crutched Friars Glasshouse in London was opened by Jean Carré.

1569   Glassworkers from L'Altare recorded at Liège (Belgium).

1570   Archduke Ferdinand II of Tyrol opened a rival glassworks to Hall-in-Tyrol in Innsbruck (Austria).

1581   The earliest mention of a glass industry at Middleburg in the Netherlands.

1602   The beginnings of the glassmaking centres in the Brandenburg area of central Drewitz near Potsdam.

1605   First mention of glass made at Nevers in France under guidance from the Altarists.

1607   The first American glasshouse established at Jamestown in Virginia.

1610   Sir George Hay established the first Scottish glasshouse at Wemyss.

1612	Publication of *L'Arte Vetraria* by Antonio Neri.
1618–1648	The Thirty Years War in which the Protestant people of Bohemia revolted against the Catholic Emperor Ferdinand II, wanting instead to be ruled by Frederic, Elector of Palatine.
1628	Coal-fired glasshouses were opened at Leith, port of Edinburgh.
1630	Sir Robert Mansell brought over the Dagnia family from L'Altare, one branch settling in Bristol (1651), the other in Newcastle-upon-Tyne (1648).
c 1638	The Bonhomme Glass Factory at Liège in Belgium was established.
1642–1648	The Civil War in England.
1653	Richard-Lucas de Nehou established a factory at Tourlaville near Cherbourg in Normandy.
1665	Jean-Baptiste Colbert established a glasshouse in the Faubourg St Antoine in Paris.
1676	Giacomo Bernardini Scapitta founded the Kungsholm Glasbruk in Stockholm.
1681	The first Finnish glasshouse established by Gustaf Jung at Nystad.
1691	The Skanska Glasbruket factory founded north of Scania.
1693	Nehou set up the Manufacture Royale des Grandes Glaces, at the Château de St Gobain in Picardy.

Early eighteenth century

	The St Petersburg Imperial Glass Factory was established (now Lenigrad) by Tsar Peter I (1682–1725).
1701	An English craftsman by the name of Tysack was brought over the Manelin to help establish the Lauensteiner Hutte glassworks in Hanover. Styles were very English, some of the early pieces being prone to crisselling. It finally closed in 1870.
1712	The Harrachov Glassworks founded at Novy Svet (Neuwelt) in northern Bohemia.
1713	The Treaty of Utrecht.
1728	The Royal Glassworks, La Granja de San Ildefonso, established south-west of Segovia in Spain under the patronage of Queen Isabella (Isabel Farnese).
1739	Caspar Wistar opened his factory in Wistarburg, Salem County, southern New Jersey, USA.
1741	The first Norwegian manufactory opened at Nöstetangen.
1742	Frederick the Great forbade the import of glass into Silesia.

Glassworks

1750	The Alloa glassworks established in Scotland soon famous for bottles decorated with quilling and decorative spattered coloured glass.
1757	The first opaque white glass made in the Bristol area, possibly at the Redcliff Backs Glasshouse.
1762	The Hadelands Glasverk founded in Norway.
1763	Henry William Stiegel (1729–85) established a glassworks at Elizabeth Furnace, Pennsylvania, USA.
1763	The Bachmetov Glass Factory founded near St Petersburg in Russia.
1764	The Baccarat Glass Factory, near Luneville in Lorraine, was founded by Monseigneur de Montmorency-Laval, producing English-style decanters.
1765	The Royal Dutch Glass Works had its beginnings at Leerdam, near Utrecht producing ordinary decanters and versions in ornamental crystal.
1767	The glassworks at St-Louis, near Bitche, in the Münzthal, Lorraine, was given the title 'Verrerie Royale de Saint-Louis' under a decree from Louis XV.
1768	Publication of Sir William Hamilton's collection of Greek vases which led to the neo-classical trend in English decanters.
1775–1783	The American War of Independence.
1776	Benjamin Edwards, Snr. opened a glasshouse in Belfast.
1778	The Vonêche glassworks were established in the Ardennes region near Namur, Belgium, under an authority granted by Empress Maria Thérèse.
1783	Phillipe-Charles Lambert founded the St-Cloud glassworks, west of Paris which was one of the first French factories to adopt the English style of glassware.
1783	Cork Glass Co, formed in Cork, Ireland.
1783	The Waterford Glass Works founded in Ireland.
1784	John Frederick Amelung founded the New Bremen Glass Manufactory, USA.
1785	Charles Mulvaney & Company was formed in Dublin.
1788	John Robert Lucas established the Nailsea glasshouse near Bristol.
1789	Outbreak of the French Revolution followed from 1792–1802 by the French Revolutionary Wars involving Austria, Prussia, Germany, Italy and the Netherlands.
c 1790	Apsley Pellat Snr. bought the Falcon Glassworks in Southwark, London passing it to his more famous son of the same name (1791–1863).
1793	The Notsjö glassworks were founded near the village of Nuutjärvi, in Finland.

16 Opposite: Excellent colour and engraving combined in this Dutch bottle-decanter which dates from the second half of the seventeenth century.

1807	The first power-driven cutting machinery introduced in Stourbridge, England.
1808	Bakewell's glasshouse opened in Pittsburgh, Pennsylvania.
1810	The Reijmyre Glassworks founded in Östergötland in Sweden.
1812	The American seaboard blockaded giving impetus to the home industry.
c 1815	Daniel Foley established the Waterloo Glass House in Cork, Ireland.
1817	Formation of the New England Glass Company at East Cambridge Massachusetts USA.
1818	Edward and Richard Ronayne opened the Terrace Glass Works in Cork, Ireland.
1821	Establishment of Choisy-le-Roi glassworks in Paris by M. Grimbolt.
1823	Joseph Lobmeyr (1792–1855) established a glasshouse in Vienna.
1825	Boston and Sandwich Glass Company formed by Deming Jarves at Sandwich, near Cape Cod, in Massachusetts.
1825	The Danish factory was established in Holmegaard's Moor on the Island of Zealand, employing German and Bohemian workers to produce tableware.
1825	The largest crystal glass works in Belgium opened at Val-Saint-Lambert, near Liège.
1825	Bakewell Pears first applied for a patent for pressed glass in America.
1828	Deming Jarves granted his first patent, USA.
1830	The Second French Revolution in which Belgium became a separate nation.
1830	McGann, a Pennsylvanian glassmaker patented a method of making decanters from pressed glass.
1833	The Eda Glassworks opened in Sweden.
1834	Founding of Conradsminde Glassworks near Aalborg in Jutland. It closed in 1857.
1834	Messrs Richardson of Stourbridge, England introduced the first machines for making pressed glass.
1834	James Powell took over the Whitefriars Glass Works.
1836	The Klostermühle glassworks opened in Bohemia, known as the Lötz factory when it was taken over by Johann Lötz (1778–1848) around 1840.
1837	Deming Jarves established the Mount Washington Glass Company in South Boston, Massachusetts.
1845	The English Glass Excise Act repealed.
1846	Christian Dorflinger (1828–1915) established the Dorflinger Glass Works at White Mills, Pennsylvania.

1847	Formation of the company of Stevens & Williams in Stourbridge. The Kastrup factory opened near Copenhagen in Denmark.
1848	The Third French Revolution and the establishment of a Republic.
1851	The Union Glass Co. opened at Somerville, Massachusetts.
1851	The Great Exhibition at Crystal Palace, London.
1858	Cape Cod Glass Company formed by Deming Jarves after he had left the Boston & Sandwich Glass Co.
c 1859	Antonio Salvati, a Venetian glassworker, founded a glasshouse in Murano.
1861–1865	The American Civil War.
c 1864	John Moncrieff founded a glassworks in Perth in Scotland.
1864	William Leighton discovered the new soda-lime formula.
1864	The Boda Glassworks established in Sweden by Scheutz and Widlund.
1867	Emile Gallé established his first glasshouse near Nancy.
1867	The Paris Exhibition which highlighted engraved glass.
1870–71	Franco-Prussian war between German States and France under Napoleon III.
1875	The formation of Daum Frères Glassworks (recently known as Cristalleries de Nancy).
1878	Paris Exhibition which highlighted experimental glass.
1878	William L. Libbey (1827–83) leased the glasswork in Toledo, Ohio, which was to become the Libbey Glass Co. in 1888.
1880	Thomas G. Hawkes & Co. founded at Corning, New York.
1881	The Iittala glassworks were founded in Finland.
1884	Paris Exhibition.
1885	Louis Comfort Tiffany (1848–1933) opened his first glasshouse in Long Island, New York with the technical help of Arthur J. Nash (1849–1934).
1889	Paris Exhibition.
1893	The Chicago World Fair.
1897	Victor Durand, Jr. (1870–1931) established the Vineland Flint Glass Works at Vineland, New Jersey, USA.
1900	Paris Exhibition.

1901   The Quezal Art Glass & Decorating Glass Company, was formed by former Tiffany
            employees Martin Bach and Thomas Johnson.

1901   H. C. Fry (1840–1929) founded his own glass company in Rochester, Pennsylvania.

1903   The Steuben Glassworks founded by Frederick Carder and T. G. Hawkes, taken over by
            the Corning Glass Co. in 1918.

1908   René Lalique (1860–1945) established a glass factory at Combs near Paris.

1910   The Riihimaki glassworks established in Finland about 70 miles from Helsinki.

1928   Arthur J. Nash (1849–1934) formed the A. Douglas Nash Corporation when his
            partnership with Tiffany broke up.

1936   Descendants of the famous fifteenth-century Murano enammeler, Anzolo Barovier (*d*
            1460) established the company of Barovier Toso.

1960   The Caithness Glass Ltd, company formed with factories at Wick and Oban, especially
            valued for their modern engraved decanters and carafes.

*17 Above left: A Russian marriage set,
nineteenth century. (Dudley Museum).*

*18 Classic Art deco decanters: the whole
emphasis of line and decoration being geometric
in the 1920s and 1930s.*

19 The earliest sealed and dated bottle to be found intact. (Central Museum and Art Gallery, Northampton).

2

The Evolution of the Decanter

Our modern decanter fulfills three roles: it is a decorative object from which to pour drinks; it is useful for temporarily storing the remains of a bottle of alcohol and it ensures that, in the case of heavy wines, the leas are separated out. But it was not always so. In the Middle Ages the last two roles did not apply. Wines and spirits were sold in large quantities. Claret from France, and 'sack', a white wine from Spain and the Canaries, would arrive in huge wooden casks; the popular German wines, known in the seventh century as 'Rhenish', would come stored in large stoneware bottles; while beer and ale would come direct from the brewery in large wooden barrels or tuns. All would be delivered straight to the large cellars of either the wine merchant or the wealthy individual who had ordered them so that, as and when required, small amounts could be tapped off and brought to the table, leaving the remainder, sealed and fresh, in the barrel. In the alehouses and taverns drink would be brought up from the cellar in the type of leather skins so frequently depicted in Breughel's paintings. For the local Lord, however, such treatment would have been unthinkable. The container from which he poured his drink would have had to have been a lavish affair of carved rock crystal, glass, silver, or even of gold, and it is in these early expensive vessels that we find the first tentative form of the decanter – the decanter-jug.

The Venetians were the first to produce glass versions of these decanter-jugs on a large scale, creating them from a wide variety of new types of glass, brilliant and fanciful enough to compete with silver, gold and rock crystal.

Decanter-bottles

The decanter-jug was the most ornate fore-runner of the modern decanter, its other much humbler relative was the bottle-decanter.

The Romans had been making use of glass for their bottles ever since the discovery of glassblowing in the first century AD, and had brought their tradition to Europe in a wide variety of shapes from globular to square, cylindrical and chamfered octagonal. When the Empire collapsed although glass production continued in northern Europe, the British wine trade had to be content with bottles and flasks made of stoneware, earthenware, or pot. It was not until the 1620s when Sir Robert Mansell took charge of the industry that the British made glass bottles on any large scale.

These early bottles however, would bear little resemblance to their modern counterparts neatly stacked in rows down in the cellar all correctly 'binned'. Binning did not come into practice until the first quarter of the eighteenth century when the cylindrical bottle was rediscovered. Prior to that the bottles of Mansell's day, known to collectors as shaft-and-globes, had spherical bases and were stored in a sand-bed on the cellar floor. The earliest ones, from 1620

20 The nineteenth-century Italian revival of earlier Venetian techniques shown to the best advantage in this handled decanter with adventurine decoration, with applied prunts and pincered ornament. (Dudley Museum).

and 1660, had long necks and a low *kick* in the base which served the dual purpose of making the bottle stable and raising the rough *pontil* mark above the surface of the table to avoid scratching. They were still more functional than attractive and it took a while before glass-blowers made a conscious attempt to make them more ornate. The movement began between 1650 and 1685. This was the period when bottles were *sealed* that is, a prunt or blob of glass was applied to either the shoulder or the body of the bottle imprinted, like a seal, with either the name of the wine merchant, the name of the customer, the date of bottling, or the name of the contents. (The bottle illustrated in Fig. 19 is an excellent example of this period, clearly stamped with the owner's initials and the date of 1657.)

Gradually more than one seal might be included, not necessarily stamped with the name or initials, but with abstract motifs. Further fancy trails of glass, ornate handles, etching and engraving could be added. Moreover the glass itself could move from the conventional browns and greens into more powerful shades ranging from blues to purples, blown in much thinner shapes. Bottle-decanters of this type, with either one or two handles, perhaps sporting a hinged metal lid, were favoured throughout Britain and Northern Europe until the middle of the eighteenth century, and were among the most popular shapes produced at Nöstentangen in the nineteenth century.

If the decanter was slow to emerge as a distinct vessel from bottles and jugs, the idea of giving it a name of its own was even slower. The first use of the word 'decant' appeared in the English language in the early seventeenth century in the works of Sir Henry Wotten (1568–1639), used in a scientific context to describe the act of pouring a liquid off from its precipitate. Application of the term to wines does not appear until much later, in an advertisement of 1690, now in the collection of the Ashmolean Museum in Oxford, which both illustrates and describes a 'Decantor' made of earthenware. Its shape is identical to the decanter-jugs which Ravenscroft had been making in glass some fifteen years before the advertisement, so one can assume that his clear-glass decanter-jugs were also being tentatively referred to as decanters by the 1680s. The term must most certainly have been in regular use by 1770 for a tariff imposed in 1701 lists 'glass bottles, Drinking glass, Decanters and all other sorts of glassware' imported from England into France as being liable for duty, while by 1715 a definition was being included in Kersey's Dictionary stating that a decanter was 'a Bottle made of Clear Flint-Glass, for the holding of Wine, etc, to be poured off into a Drinking-Glass.'

The decanter may have emerged as a new vessel in its own right, but it certainly did not immediately oust the bottle for the serving of wine at table. The two seem to have co-existed happily for at least the next hundred years. As late as the nineteenth century large numbers of gaily-coloured Nailsea and Alloa decanter-bottles were still being produced. By the mid-nineteenth century, however, it was generally accepted that an ornate decanter, rather than a bottle, was the only fitting container for the serving of table wines in well-bred society. The last struggles of the contest for table dominance was best summed up by the 'black bottle incident' of the 1850s. At the centre of the dispute was none other than Lord Cardigan (1797–1868), the man who was to lead the Light Brigade in that fateful charge of 1854. Cardigan was a stickler for discipline and propriety and when, one evening in the mess, he observed one of his young officers pouring his wine at table from a bottle, as opposed to a decanter, he was so appalled that he banned the young gentleman from future meals with his fellow officers, unless he was prepared to apologize. The young man was not, and when details of the incident leaked out to the press there was a huge outcry against Cardigan. Whenever the General appeared

21 *Ravenscroft syllabub decanter-jug, sold for £2,500 at Phillips, Son & Neale in May 1974. Height 10¹/₈ in.*

in public he was met with loud taunts and jeers of 'black bottle, black bottle'. The Crimean War, however, interrupted the dispute. The young officer was one of the six hundred who rode into the 'jaws of death' never to return and the matter was never resolved. However, one can safely say that by the mid-nineteenth century polite society had banned the bottle from the table. The decanter had come into its own.

The evolution of the decanter in Britain was a reflection of what had been happening throughout Europe. Initially, each country showed a market preference for their own particular type of decanter-jug or decanter-bottle depending on how technically advanced their glass industry was. By the mid-eighteenth century, however, these localized differences were being eroded. New decanter shapes were soon universally adopted throughout Europe, and the recently established American industry was soon imitating them across the other side of the Atlantic. The early nineteenth century marked the beginning of a brisk international glass trade which gathered momentum at such a rate that shapes and methods of decoration began to diversify again. Decanters of completely different shapes, styles, and decorative forms were available concurrently throughout Europe and America – a situation which has continued to the present day.

The ensuing list of decanter types is an attempt to trace the origin and development of decanter shape and includes as much detail as possible to help with dating. It is only at the end of the nineteenth century and on into the twentieth century that decanters become so diverse that listing becomes impractical. As a further aid to categorization the numerical prefix to each type indicates the century in which it first appeared, the letters of the alphabet being used to delineate the approximate order in which the various types evolved.

16a

TYPE 16a: THE EWER DECANTER

This shape was popular throughout Europe from Spain and Venice through France and Germany from the Middle Ages onwards. The Venetians, from the late fifteenth century found it an excellent vehicle for their lace-like *latticino* glass. By the seventeenth century it had become popular in France where glass-makers frequently made it of mottled coloured glass and it was also one of the first shapes to be made at Nöstetangen in the 1760 to 1770 period, when decoration would take the *façon de Venise* trailed and twisted ornamentation, the long-shanked stopper in the form of a solid glass ball as in the example illustrated.

TYPE 16b: THE KUTTROLF SPIRIT DECANTER

A popular form of decanter in Germany during the sixteenth and seventeenth centuries, the bulbous body connected to the pouring mouth by four thin intertwined tubes which terminated in a wide, sometimes pan-shaped mouth. The fact that the tubes were of such thin diameter meant that the liquid poured extremely slowly. The fashion spread from Germany to Holland and Scandinavia during the late eighteenth century, the Dutch and Swedes preferring a more upright version either in the shape of a double gourd (as illustrated) from the

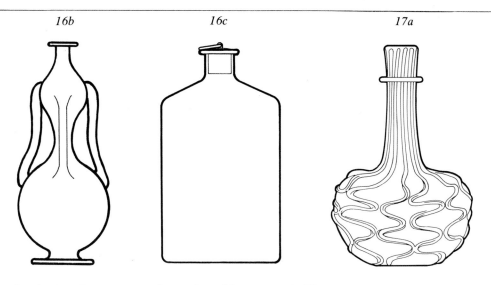

early nineteenth century or from the mid-nineteenth century with the tubes travelling up vertically from the base to give an almost cylindrical outline. Still popular today, they are known in Scandinavia as *Kluk-Kluk* decanters owing to the fact that the liquid makes a clucking sound as it is poured. In the nineteenth century these upright versions were being made by the Stourbridge firm of Stevens and Williams decorated with solid ball stopper and applied prunts and rigarees.

TYPE 16c: THE EARLY SPIRIT DECANTER
This was popular first in Germany and Bohemia in the late sixteenth century where spirits of all kind were widely drunk. The squares, often only slightly larger than bottles were easy to pack in luggage and were equally attractive for use on sideboard or table. The fact that they were given such elaborate enamelled and *schwarzlot* decoration would mean that they were certainly intended for bedside table use as well as when travelling. In England, square decanter shapes did not appear until about 1750, slightly tapering to the base to facilitate removal from the two-part mould. In Sweden and North Holland, uncut clear enamelled squares were extremely numerous from the end of the eighteenth century as containers for the widely-consumed *aquavit*. They were not usually made with a glass stopper, but rather with a cork fitted with a silver or silver-plate pull-ring finial. Similar versions with pewter stoppers were also the pride of Stiegel in America, enamelled in up to six colours which were far fresher and brighter than their European counterparts.

TYPE 17a: THE EARLY BOTTLE-DECANTER
Popular in England until about 1720, the main characteristic of the bottle-decanter was the *string-rim* placed towards the top of the neck and intended to act as an anchor for the string which was used to bind the cork in place and keep the contents sealed. Bottle-decanters closely imitated the shape of the binning bottles of the time with long neck and knife-edged string rim prior to 1650, more shouldered and incurving at the base from 1650 to 1680, and much wider and squatter with tapering neck from 1680 to 1715. The body of the decanter was frequently ornamented by tooled decoration, especially the nipped diamond waies. Height ranged from six and a half inches to ten inches, and most frequently the glass would be amethyst or yellowish brown in colour. Ravenscroft's 1677 price list also states that the bottles could also 'have stoppers fitted to them' if required, but few have stood the test of time.

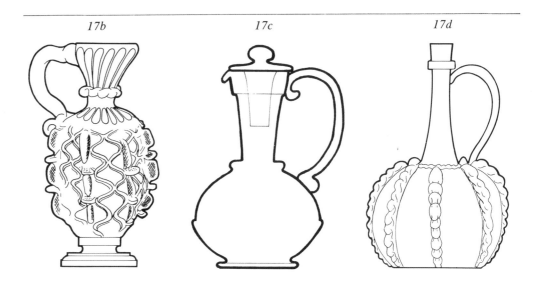

TYPE 17b: THE RAVENSCROFT DECANTER-JUG

This was the earliest type of English decanter-jug, developed at the time of Ravenscroft's newly-discovered lead-glass. It remained popular throughout the 1670–1700 period. The handle and the ornamentation of the body would be in the form of *façon de Venise* nipped, pinched and trailed decoration. Towards the end of the century the foot rim became less pronounced and the body, instead of tapering inwards, had almost vertical sides, with heavy moulded decoration. Examples are rarely found together with stopper, probably due to the fact that they were meant for the serving of thick mulled drinks made with cream, oats, and bread or effervescent drinks like cider, beer and ale. The kick, slightly raised on the base of the decanter was retained to hide the rough pontil mark.

TYPE 17c: THE RAVENSCROFT CLARET JUG

Popular in England throughout the same period as TYPE 17b, a frequent characteristic of TYPE 17c was a wide vertically-sided mouth known as a *pan-lip* which tapered to a small spout conducive to the pouring of wine. The neck opening was large to facilitate filling direct from the flask without use of a funnel. Originally, most of these examples would have been made with a loose-fitting stopper, with a long shank descending fairly far down into the decanter neck to act as an anchor. The foot was folded over underneath both to hide the pontil mark and to give an added thickness to resist wear and tear. Handles, as in TYPE 17b, were basically swan-shaped sometimes with a pinched thumb-hold fashioned at the top to facilitate pouring.

TYPE 17d: THE FLAGON DECANTER

In this version the string rim is retained, the neck becomes much taller, the body is blown to much cleaner lines, and the body fitted with one or two swan-shaped handles extending from shoulder to just below the string rim. This type had been popular in the Netherlands since *c* 1600 often fitted, from about 1625 with a hinged tin lid. An example in the Museum Lambert van Meerten in green glass, with thumb rest on the handle, bears the inscription 'Let the Glass Go Round' on a seal attached to the front of the body. The shape remained popular there into the eighteenth century, with a more globular body, the string-rim tooled and the small pouring lip fashioned at the rim. Often twin-handled, the body would also be decorated in Venetian trails, the whole standing on a rimmed foot. In England this style (usually featuring only one handle, and frequently in soft brown

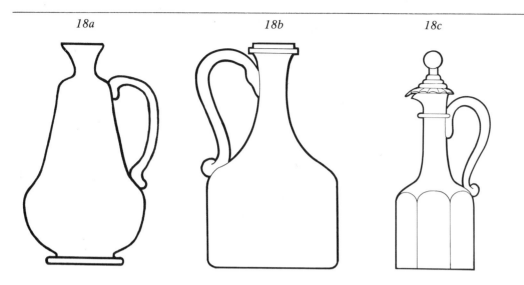

amethyst glass), was the successor to the Ravenscroft decanter-jug when it disappeared around 1710. By about 1740 to 1750 the string-rim was no longer angular, but now took the form of tooled decoration as on the Dutch decanter-jugs of a slightly earlier date. In England, the flagon decanter was finally eclipsed by the new tapered decanters of the 1760s, but in Norway it was particularly popular at Nöstetangen from the 1820s onwards, where flagon decanters, heavily decorated with trailed ornament were known as *'Zirat flaske'*.

TYPE 18a: THE PYRIFORM DECANTER-JUG
Another uniquely Scandinavian shape which appeared at a much earlier date, around 1715. Like the Ravenscroft decanter the wide mouth and distinctively bulbous body meant that it was ideal as a container for the warming thickened drinks served on dark winter evenings.

TYPE 18b: QUEEN ANNE CYLINDER
DECANTER
This straight-sided type evolved soon after 1700 at about the same time as the first cylinder wine bottles. In early specimens the kick is high and cone-shaped, gradually disappearing as the shape began to fall out of fashion about 1730. The usual type of

stopper from 1710 onwards would have been solid, the ball finial perhaps with a single tear-shaped bubble trapped inside it as decoration. Gradually the string-rim climbed up the neck until it became little more than a decorative lip. In the 1720 to 1730 period all decanters were made with a small bevel at the top of the neck where the decanter had been snapped off the rod.

Unfortunately for the collector few of these early Queen Anne pieces have survived. As has been seen from the historical outline, the early years of Anne's reign were marred by the War of the Spanish Succession. Trade relations between England and France were strained. Heavy fine duties at the staggering rate of £55 per tun, were levied on imported champagne and French wines from 1703 onwards. Despite the fact that Portuguese wines still managed to get through taxed at the much lighter rate of £7 per tun, English drinking habits were forced to change. Gradually spirits, cider, or strong ale began to take the place of the popular French wines. Presumably, therefore, there may not have been such a great demand for wine decanters during Anne's reign.

TYPE 18c: THE QUEEN ANNE MALLET
DECANTER
This was the type popular in the more

restrained Queen Anne period, after the exuberance of the Restoration in England. Introduced around 1700, it remained popular until into the 1730 by which time the handle had been abandoned. The main features are the six or eight-sided body, the steeply-sloping shoulder, and the fact that the neck is almost as long as the body. The string-rim took on a variety of shapes, rounded, knife-edged, single or treble, depending on the whim of the maker, as it was now only a decorative form and served no useful purpose. Where the decoration is tooled out of the neck no join appears on the vertical line of the ring, whereas rings applied of molten glass will alway show the signs of overlapping where the trails were joined together. By 1710 however the spout and the ornate stopper faded from fashion.

TYPE 18d: THE QUATREFOIL DECANTER

The quatrefoil was an interesting variation of the mallet decanter, appearing in both pint and quart sizes, and was popular from about 1725 to 1760. During this period it was considered the height of fashion to serve both red and white wines chilled after standing them, together with the glasses, in a large silver or ceramic bowl containing ice. Wine in the conventional mallets did not cool well because the large diameter of the body precluded uniform temperature. The Quatrefoil, or cruciform decanter, however, with its cruciform cross-section, meant that the cooling effect could rapidly reach the contents at the centre of the decanter. Often these decanters were accompanied by large ball stoppers of solid glass which, from *c* 1725, were decorated with tear-shaped bubbles trapped within the glass. There was still no attempt to make the stopper fit the everted mouth.

TYPE 18e: THE CONICAL DECANTER-JUG

This was the type widely produced at the Swedish glasshouse at Skänska Glasbruket from about 1740 onwards. Much earlier versions had been produced around Amiens from the first century AD but the Swedes made it their own, decorating it with line engraving, or enamelling on clear colourless glass. The same shape also occurs without the handle as a simple carafe. In the 1860s and 1870s the conical decanter caught the eye of Thomas Webb in England and several were made in clear uncoloured glass with added *façon de Venise* trailing.

TYPE 18f: THE BOHEMIAN DECANTER-BOTTLE

Based on the much earlier pilgrim bottle, this shape was popular from about 1720 in

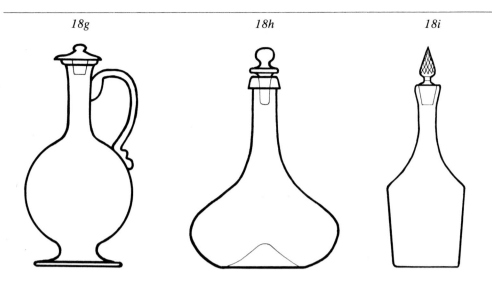

18g   18h   18i

Bohemia and Germany, the ovoid or bulbous onion shape ideal for their fine engravings of mythological and classical scenes. The footrim on this bottle shape was of uniquely European taste. The squat neck was often ornamented with shallow-cut circles or ovals and the underpart of the body with shallow rounded flutes, leaving the body free for the main engraved motifs. Initially, the bottles would have been sold with silver or silver-plated corks, but by 1750 the faceted spire stopper was in wide use. In England, the shape appeared towards the end of the nineteenth century, when the art of engraving was at its height, frequently fitted with silver neck ring and silver stopper. A fine example, as late as 1920, was a green glass decanter made by James Powell and sons of Blackfriars engraved with a wreath of ferns.

TYPE 18g: THE SPANISH DECANTER-JUG

This style became particularly popular at La Granja de San Ildefonso about 1775. The body was either of ovoid or bulbous circular section, the stopper, reminiscent of the early Ravenscroft decanters, loosely fitting with a ball finial, and the handle in the form of a *façon de Venise* snake. Examples are mostly of crystal, either cut, with fire-gilt decoration, engraved or decorated with coloured enamelling of floral motifs. As the

Spanish Empire spread, so this shape went with them, numerous examples being made in Mexico where the stopper was replaced by a hinged pewter lid.

TYPE 18h: THE SHAFT-AND-GLOBE DECANTER

About 1735 the string-rim began to disappear from the neck of the decanter, along with the decorative ring around the base of the neck and the handle. The result was a more streamlined version of the bottle decanter with tall slender neck and globular body. As early as 1675, a glass-maker by the name of John Worlidge had described a method of grinding the stopper together with the interior of the mouth of the decanter to ensure a close fit, but the practice did not catch on until the 1720s and was only widely in use from the 1740s. A later advertisement of 1758 states that Frederick Stanton of London was charging 1/4d for grinding stoppers and cutting the bases of two decanters, which implies that perhaps earlier decanters were being given the latest cut and ground treatment. The shaft-and-globe remained popular until about 1775. By 1740 it was usual for the mouth of the decanter to be melted over to give a better finish, but it was not until 1750 that the first shallow lips appeared, getting much larger from 1760 onwards. As early as the 1680s

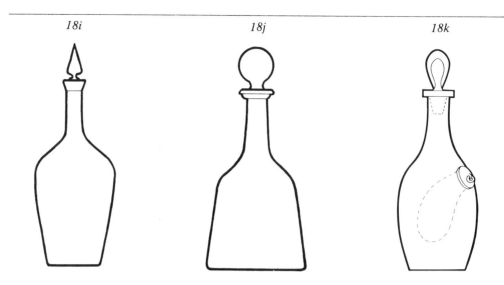

this type had been popular in Holland, especially as a vehicle for the calligraphic type of engraving of artists like Willem van Heemskerk. The Dutch would frequently make use of a hinged tin stopper attached to the neck by a circling band of tin as with the bottle decanter-jug. This type, however, is unknown in England, the most popular early form of stopper, from 1735, being one with a large glass ball-finial, or, from about 1750 with a spire stopper, as illustrated. Shallow diamond faceting on the necks of this and other later eighteenth-century types began about 1745, continuing to around 1770.

TYPE 18i: THE SHOULDER DECANTER

Popular in Austria, Germany and Bohemia from *c* 1750, the tapering cylindrical body leant itself ideally to gilt, enamel or engraved decoration. Usually, the body was blown in thickish glass, especially when intended for faceted and engraved decoration. In England, the shape appeared first around the 1740s, the shoulder having a much more rounded contour, and the glass blown to delicate thinness. It remained popular until around 1880. The new delicacy of glass was the result of a new type of furnace patented by a Bristol maker, Humphrey Perrot, in 1735, which transformed

the basic lead-glass batch from a sluggish metal to one which was easy to manipulate. Around the same time a new type of annealing was introduced which made use of the tunnel leer (from the German *'leer ofen'* meaning empty furnace). Annealing is an essential element of the glass-making process in that it ensures the stability and durability of the glass. Glass cools without annealing at different rates. Stress then sets in and the glass is prone to crack or fracture. In the tunnel leer process, the finished article was reheated in an empty furnace and then left to cool down very slowly resulting in much greater stability. Between them the combined forces of the improved furnace and the new tunnel leer opened new vistas for the glass-maker. The basic ingredients of flint-glass were not altered in any way and it still retained its characteristic brilliance and light-refracting qualities, but now it was both tougher and more easy to manipulate. Decanters could be blown of much thinner glass and still be strong enough to take cutting and engraving, hence for the first time glass-men were able to blow thin shouldered decanters. It came complete with a new style of stopper as well. The Ravenscroft stoppers had been hollow-blown with gadroon moulding; the early eighteenth-century versions had been pinched in the solid; the new shoulder

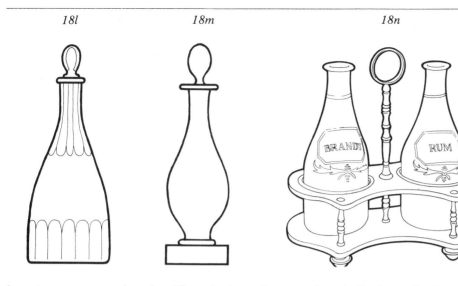

decanters came equipped with a 'spire stopper' which was almost pear or cone-shaped. From 1740 this would be plain and from 1750 faceted. The shoulder was eclipsed from the 1760s in England by the softer tapered shapes, but it re-emerged a hundred years later in the mid-Victorian period in both England and America.

TYPE 18j: THE BELL-SHAPE DECANTER

This version of the shoulder decanter flaring outwards from the shoulder to the base creating a shape reminiscent of a hand-bell, evolved in England in the late 1750s, and was usually accompanied, after 1760, by a flat, circular, disc stopper, which, after the 1770s might be shallow cut round the edges if the main body of the decanter was engraved with shallow cut motifs. From the mid-eighteenth century stopper ends were ground flat to obliterate the tool marks.

TYPE 18k: THE CHAMPAGNE DECANTER

This new shape, from the 1750s, was the successor to the quatrefoil decanter in Britain. This time, however, the cooling was achieved by filling the compartment, blown into the side of the decanter, with crushed ice. Similar decanters, known as *Kühl-flasche*, were produced in Germany about

the same time, in the form of a decanter jug accompanied by solid ball-finial stopper. Unfortunately, in both instances the practicality of the decanter was outweighed by its intrinsic ungainliness and by the 1780s it was falling into disfavour.

TYPE 18l: THE TAPERED DECANTER

This much more elegant shape in tune with the new rococo taste, began to appear in England about 1765. With it came a new lozenge-shaped stopper. It was a shape very popular with the Bristol manufacturers of coloured glass. In clear glass, after about 1768, the most usual form of decoration was vertical fluting around the neck and a herringbone fringe of finer cuts around the base leaving the body free for further decoration. The same type with a herringbone fringe had reached Bohemia by the late 1780s where the body would be covered from shoulder to base by fluting and diamond cuts around a central monogrammed medallion. The Spanish adopted it from about 1775 decorating it with delicate rococo fire-gilt engraving. At the Swedish Småland glasshouses the fluting was omitted and the body decorated with wheel-engraving, whilst the French decorated it with gilding around the rim and shoulder in the Louis XVI style.

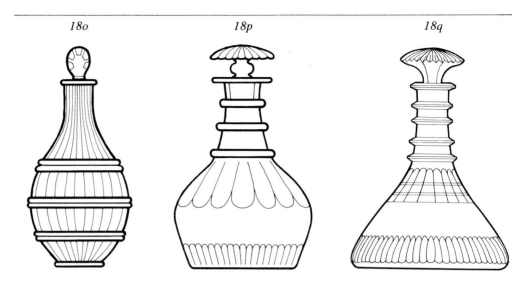

TYPE 18m: THE CORDIAL DECANTER

This shape was a complete reflection of the Adam style and was popular in England from the 1780s on into the Regency period. Early decoration took the form of classically draped festoons, but after the turn of the century motifs became much fussier. Cordial, a popular ladies' drink from the 1770s onwards, was slightly less potent than present-day liqueurs and sipped only in small quantities. Earliest examples might be blown into two, three or four shapes fused together so that the decanter was divided into four separate compartments each having individual spouts branching from the same communal neck. In this way several different types of cordial could be stored in the same decanter. Cordial decanters were often made from clear glass so that the drinks could be recognized by their various colours, but occasionally coloured glass examples are found with the names of the contents written on the outside of each compartment either in gilt or enamel lettering. In France the same shape was delicately decorated with gilt neo-classical motifs.

TYPE 18n: DECANTER STANDS

Stands of this type first began to appear around 1765 to house the popular coloured Bristol glass decanters with their gilt labels. The stands would be made of silver, silver plate, brass, wood, or even *papier mâché*, with a central pole topped by a handle, in these eighteenth-century Bristol examples, to carry them. The decanters were rarely accompanied by glass stoppers, but instead would have had cork stoppers topped with material matching the stand. About 1880 the coloured glass decanters fell out of favour, and in their place sets of facet-cut cylindrical decanters would be housed in a circular stand of silver or Sheffield plate, perhaps with a cut glass bowl for ice suspended from the carrying pole. An interesting novel version of the decanter-stand, the decanter-waggon, had a sudden burst of popularity in the 1820 to 1830 era. It was designed by George IV, after whom the Regency style had been named, and was an ingenious way around the court ruling that the port must never be passed by hand in front of the King, which had meant that, prior to the invention of the waggon, the guest on His Majesty's left-hand side was expected to rise and pass the decanter behind the King's back to the guest on the right. The prototype, in silver gilt, was made to the King's specifications by Sir Edward Thomason of Birmingham, and later presented by the King to the Duke of Wellington. In their turn these waggon decanters were succeeded, about 1840, by

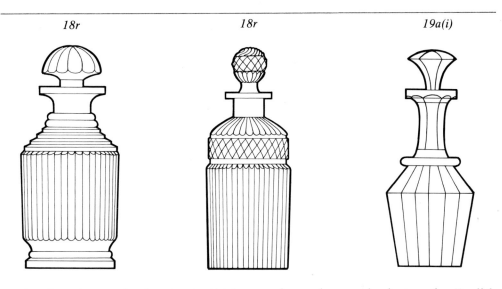

much taller, elegant circular stands which housed thin tapering cylinder decanters with spire stoppers. The final form of decanter stand was the *tantalus*, so called because the three square decanters were housed in a wooden stand fitted with a bar which could be locked across the stopper. Only the master of the house would have the key. Other members of the household wanting to steal a quick nip would be tantalized by being able to see the contents of the decanters but unable to remove the stoppers because of the locked bar.

TYPE 18o: THE BARREL-DECANTER

In 1775, Christopher Heady, a Bath glass-maker, advertised the arrival of 'Curious barrel-shaped decanters cut on an entirely new pattern'. It is now generally accepted by the experts that the shape referred to is of TYPE 18o in which vertical cuts down the length of the body represented the wooden staves of a wine barrel while the horizontal circles cut at regular intervals around the body and neck represented the hoops. This shape was extremely popular with the Baccarat factory in France who were producing it in the same 1780–1790 period. French and Dutch versions, however, can be distinguished from the English in that the European examples are of soda glass with the pontil

mark rough-ground whereas the English had developed means of smoothing and polishing the base of their decanters. The fore-runner of the barrel-decanter, without the hoop and stave cutting, is generally known as the Indian-club decanter. It was thinly blown and frequently engraved with fruiting vines or cartouche labels stating the contents.

TYPE 18p: THE PRUSSIAN DECANTER

This shape was extensively illustrated in English advertisements from the 1780s onwards when it was referred to as the 'Prussian'. The main characteristics of the Prussian are the three widely-spaced neck rings (which facilitated a good grip while pouring) a wide mouth with a very pronounced lip, a broad-shouldered bulbous body with a pronounced inward slope to the base, and a completely new mushroom stopper. The shape is presumed to be based on the bulbous beer barrels of the period, and some would argue that this is the shape which Christopher Heady claimed to have invented, although this is unlikely. The shape was immensely popular up until the 1830s and was widely imitated throughout Europe up until the 1840s, and as late as the 1850s and 1860s in America. Early pieces were thickly blown, but towards the turn of the century the metal became thicker to

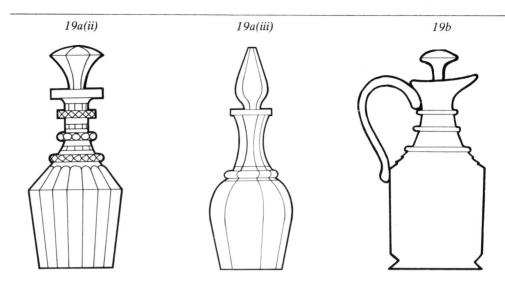

take the deeper cut designs which were applied to it. Sizes ranged from miniaturized salesman's samples, barely $3\frac{1}{2}$ inches tall through the spirit and wine sizes to the various large sizes: the magnum (two quarts), the Jeroboam (four bottles), the Rehoboam (six bottles) up to the largest size (holding twenty-one bottles) which was recorded by Cecil Davis as being owned by the late André Simon and exhibited at the Wine Trade Festival. The mushroom stopper was the most usual accompaniment, but in the early stages of its development it might be accompanied by target or bull's eye stoppers, while from the 1820s heavily cut globe or pinnacle stoppers might be used. It is interesting to note that European and American versions of the Prussian frequently incorporate a foot-rim, an ornament which was never adopted by the Anglo-Irish.

TYPE 18q: THE 'RODNEY' SHIP'S DECANTER
This was the English maritime version of the Prussian shape and first appeared about 1780, named after the English Admiral Rodney who had successfully beaten both the French and Spanish fleets in the 1780s. It had the same mushroom stopper and fluting patterns as the Prussian, the main differences being the additional neck rings and the pronounced conical shape which, hav-

ing a low centre of gravity, meant that it was unlikely to tip over in rough weather. Prior to its introduction ship's decanters had been given completely circular bases and were housed in straw or wicker-work baskets so that they could be hung from a beam in the captain's cabin.

TYPE 18r: THE CYLINDER DECANTER
The early cylinder decanter, which began to emerge in England some time between 1790 and the turn of the century, had vertical sides and simple ball or target stoppers. Neck rings were retained until about 1815, but then they were abandoned with the new fashion for prismatic cutting. Around 1830 pillar-reeding came back into fashion, the body from shoulder to base cut with deep vertical grooves to create a series of rounded pillars.

TYPES 19a: 'THE ROYAL', THE 'NELSON'
AND 'THE FANCY'.
These were the last three definite shapes of the Anglo-Irish period, the decoration relying heavily on broad bands of faceting or fluting. Introduced about 1828, the characteristics were the straight-sided inward-sloping body and the matching fluting on the tall stoppers. Usually there were between twelve and fourteen flutes extending up the body. At the Baccarat factory in

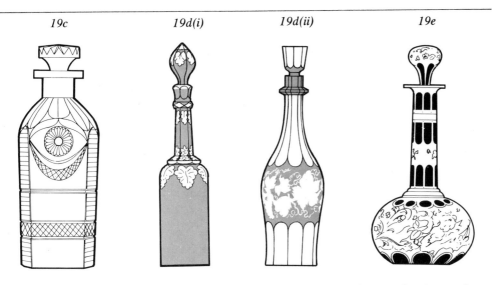

19c   *19d(i)*   *19d(ii)*   *19e*

France this same shape, without the neck-rings, was used with a band of diamonds circling the body below the shoulder in a drinking service for King Louis-Phillipe. By 1840, in England, the angular shoulder had been rounded and the neck-rings had disappeared.

TYPE 19b: THE GEORGIAN CLARET DECANTER

Claret had become an expensive luxury in England during the eighteenth century as a result of the Methuen Treaty of 1703 which decreed that the duty on Portuguese wines should be less by one third than that on French wines. By Georgian times, however, the restrictions had been lifted and claret was back in popularity. The earliest claret decanters date from about 1815 and were elaborately cut in the Anglo-Irish tradition. The wide pouring lip remained a feature of claret decanters throughout the nineteenth century, the spout gradually becoming deeper. Heavy ball stoppers came into use about 1830 and by 1850 the straight cylindrical sides had been abandoned in favour of a more classical, almost urn-shaped body, tapering in sharply at the base, and then flaring out to rest on a circular foot. In France, the Georgian Claret was a popular shape at the Baccarat factory, the bulbous body cut with distinctive draped curved

motifs. The French restrained use of cutting, as compared to the cluttered late Anglo-Irish decoration, led to a much more elegant and sophisticated line. A rare version of the claret decanter of this later period is the stirrup decanter in which the urn-shaped body was left without a foot to rest on. Instead it would have been placed, along with a set of footless glasses, in a wooden stand used for serving drinks to the hunt.

TYPE 19c: THE GEORGIAN SQUARE DECANTER

Between the early Germanic square decanter and the heavily-cut Victorian tantalus decanter, the TYPE 19c transitional phase evolved in the early 1800s, the corners slightly chamfered and a combination of various cuts ornamenting the clear glass body. A few earlier examples had been made about 1745, much plainer 'squares' blown – moulded and slightly tapering towards the base, but port, rather than whisky was the predominant eighteenth-century drink and there was not much call for spirit 'squares'. Another type, popular in Regency times were the square label decanters produced in the Bristol range of amethyst, green, or blue colours with gilt decoration on the stopper and shoulder.

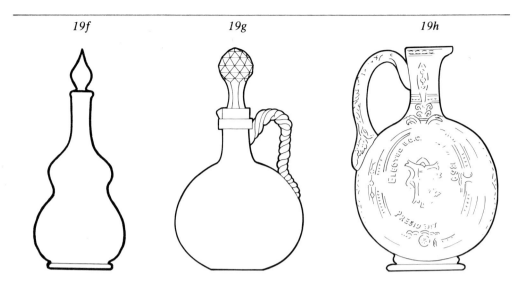

After the heavier cut squares of the Victorian period this lighter Georgian square was again revived in the Edwardian period when it sported a mushroom stopper with pronounced fluting, a faceted shoulder, and a diamond-cut base.

TYPE 19d: THE VICTORIAN FANCY CYLINDER

From the 1840s onwards decanters in England were much taller than before, with elongated stoppers giving an added elegance. The basic shape was cylindrical as in TYPE 19d(i) but other versions were made with slight waists, broadened shoulders, or, as in TYPE 19d(ii) with slightly bulbous bodies. The overall shape, however, is reminiscent of the present-day hock bottle. These were the types particularly favoured for the colourful Bohemian flashed and cased-glass decanters. It was about this time too that a much more elongated version of the 181 taper came back into fashion, the body shallow cut to give the impression of hoops and staves.

TYPE 19e: THE VICTORIAN SHAFT-AND-GLOBE

Most Victorian shaft-and-globes date from the 1850s and were frequently decorated with deep cuts in the Biedermeier cased and flashed tradition. The neck of these Victorian shaft-and-globes were much taller and the bodies much squatter than the earlier eighteenth-century versions. Stoppers were conventionally either ball, rounded, mushroom or spire-shaped. Apsley Pellatt of London exhibited a very restrained cut version in colourless crystal at the 1851 Crystal Palace Exhibition and by 1870 similar ones were being produced at the Kosta glassworks in Sweden while much later in America the shaft-and-globe was a popular shape for brilliant cutting, occasionally through cranberry glass to clear in the Beidermeier style.

TYPE 19f: THE PYRIFORM DECANTER

Another bulbous-bodied shape to appear around 1880 was the ungainly pear-shaped decanter, topped by a long-shanked hollow circular stopper. In some instances the base would be strengthened by the addition of a foot-rim. In England firms like Richardson and Powell made extensive use of the shape in their free-blown *façon de Venise* clear colourless glass decanters, while in America versions were blown in iridescent glass.

TYPE 19g: THE VICTORIAN CLARET

Claret jugs of this shape were at their height of popularity in the 1880s, many hundreds of workmen being employed to engrave

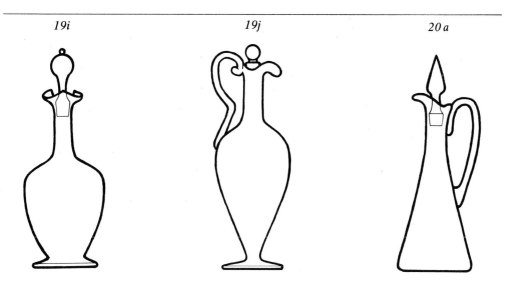

them in and around Stourbridge. In America smaller versions, about eight inches high, were known as 'whisky jugs' and were often decorated with a variety of brilliant cuts at Dorflinger and T.G. Hawkes.

TYPE 19h: THE VICTORIAN OVOID DECANTER-JUG

This was an excellent vehicle for the revived interest in engraving which was at its height in England in the 1880s. The shape was very similar to that of the Bohemian version of the 1720s (TYPE 18f), the decoration appearing in circular cartouches on either side of the body. Stoppers were optional.

TYPE 19i: THE NEO-CLASSICAL DECANTER

From about 1850 there was a gradual return to classical shapes, a fashion which was at its height by 1875. The foot-rim now became more pronounced, separated from the body by a small, pedestal-like structure. The mouth of the decanter took on the trefoil shape of the Greek *oenochoë*. Handles, when used, were of the trailed Venetian type, often raised above the mouth of the vessel, reminiscent of the Venetian ewers which had been popular in the sixteenth and early seventeenth centuries. It was widely imitated in Europe and America and

was afforded a wide variety of decorative treatments.

TYPE 19j: THE URN-SHAPED VICTORIAN DECANTER

This shape was universally popular from the 1880s onwards lending itself perfectly to the engraved and etched decorations so popular in England at the time, to the ornate brilliant-cut at Baccarat, the delicate gilding at St Louis and the revived cutting at English firms like Stevens and Williams.

TYPE 20a: THE EDWARDIAN CLARET DECANTER

As a complete revolt against the sumptuous curves of the late nineteenth-century neo-classicism, the early 1900s was a period of return to straight lines. Claret decanters were uniformly tapered outwards from just below the tip to give an overall conical shape. Frequently there would be silver neck-rings perhaps also accompanied by a silver handle and silver stopper. Frederick Carder designed this type of decanter-jug for Stevens and Williams, while in the States Steuben provided T.G. Hawkes and Co. with blanks for them to decorate further with the American brilliant cut.

Glossary of the main decorative movements

BAROQUE (1660s to 1730s)
This was a revolt against earlier Renaissance classicism and was started about 1600 by the artist Giovanni Lorenzo Bernini. On decanters its expression is to be found in the florid, curved motifs engraved by the German and Bohemian craftsmen. Every inch of the decanter would be covered with detail, a frequent framework to the main decoration being *laub-und bandelwerk* strapwork and interlacing leaf motifs. On the early spirit decanters (TYPE 16c) the same baroque spirit was shown in the enamelled and *schwarzlot* motifs which completely covered the surface of the opaque glass.

ROCOCO (1715–1774)
The term was not introduced until the early nineteenth century, but it refers to a style specifically created at the Court of Louis XV as a reaction to the heaviness of baroque designs and motifs. In the early years the complicated patterns, involving drapes, urns and balustrades, were widely copied from the design books of Jean Bérain by the German and Bohemian engravers and used to decorate the 18f TYPE of decanter-bottle.

As the style developed these early cluttered designs became much simpler, the Silesians preferring wheel-engraving based on the main-rococo period themes of asymmetrical cartouches, rocks, pierced shell-work and opposing C-scrolls. *Chinoiserie*, the European version of Chinese decoration, with its landscapes of pagodas, oriental figures and fantastical beasts, was another favourite rococo theme of the Germans and Bohemians. In painted and enamelled work, inspiration was drawn from the paintings of the French artist Antoine Watteau (1684–1742). In England the rococo influence on decanters was not so marked. The

22 Victorian fancy shapes complete with ornate steeple stoppers and Biedermeier decoration.

assymetrical fruiting vine motif and the new, more delicately blown decanters from the post-1760 period reflect its presence, but it is most marked in the exotic birds and pheasants motif of James Giles' gilt decoration and the rustic gardens and classical ruins enamelled towards the end of the Beilby period.

NEO-CLASSICAL (1760s to 1830s)
This new style, which looked to ancient Greece and Rome for its inspiration, was the result of the 1748 excavation of Pompeii which revived the taste for classical styles. In England, it is subdivided into the Adam style (from 1760) and the Regency style (1800–1830) and in France into the Louis Seize (1774–1793) followed by the Empire Style (1800–1820). The Adam and Louis Seize styles were very similar, decanters in both England and France tending towards the softer line of the bell and the taper, and ornamented with delicately diamond-point engraved festoons, urns and masks in England, and similar gilt and enamel decoration in France. The cordial decanter, resting on its classically styled pediment is typical of this period. By the turn of the century, however, in both England and France, neo-classicism had become more ornate. The excessive use of pillar fluting in England, and that of gilding on Regency Bristol Glass are typical of the later period, while in France the Empire-style cut-glass decanters began to adopt the Grecian urn-shapes mounted on pedestals, with decoration frequently featuring Egyptian motifs, following the successful campaigns of the Napoleonic Wars.

BEIDERMEIER (1820–1840)
In complete contrast to the French and English neo-classical movement the German, Bohemians and Austrian glass industries created a lavish new form of richly coloured glass to cater for the taste of the new middle-classes who had suddenly become affluent in the wake of the Napoleonic Wars. The period drew its

54

name from two characters called Bieder-
mann and Bummelmeier who had been
created by German satirist Ludwig Eich-
rodt to epitomize the new bourgeoisie.
Flashed and cased decanters became more
and more ornate as the period progressed
and were to be widely imitated by the
Americans and the rest of Europe throughout the mid-nineteenth century.

ART NOUVEAU (1880–1920)
This movement arose almost spontane-
ously throughout Europe around the 1880s
and heralded a new era of fantasy and
invention which reacted strongly against
the uniformity of mass-production. In Britain the style had its roots in the Arts and
Crafts Movement with men like William
Morris specifically commissioning decanter
designs which would have to be free-blown
and hand-decorated. Main impetus for the
glass movement was to be found in France
with the work of Eugène Rousseau and
Emile Gallé and the extensive use of etched
and cameo techniques. In America, Tiffany
extended the movement into the realms of
iridescent glass, soon to be imitated back in
Europe by the Lötz factory in Kloster-
muhle. The name for the style comes from
'Maison de l'Art Nouveau', the Parisian
interior design gallery which opened in
1896 and soon became the shop window for
Art Nouveau objects from all over the
world. The various names for the same
movement in Europe are the *Jungendstil*
in Germany, the Catalan *Modernista* and
the Viennese *Sezessionsstil*.

ART DECO (1920s and 30s)
This period was the complete opposite of
the individual free-flowing Art Nouveau
look. Instead the Art Deco movement
returned to extensive use of the straight line
and the geometric shape. In decanters this
feeling was interpreted by angular shapes
simplicity of cut, and the simple juxtaposi-
tion of colourless and coloured clear glass.

SWEDISH MODERN (1917–   )
The term applied to Swedish glass, especially from the Kosta glassworks where the
emphasis is again on individual pieces,
either beautifully engraved in great detail,
or of completely new types of glass like
Graal, Ariel and Ravenna.

23 The geometric shape of modern glass.

3

Façon de Venise and the New Metals

The creation of a decanter, be it in any of the styles just discussed, is a highly-skilled combination of technology and craftsmanship. The technologist's skill lies in the creation of the metal. By addition of oxides and alkalis, he can either produce a glass which has the crystal clearness of a mountain stream, the glittering transparency of precious stones, the opacity of milk, the iridescence of peacock's wing, or the muddy striations of semi-precious stones. The metal can be strong and heavy and ideal for carving and cutting, or it can have an ephemeral delicacy which defies the use of any further ornamentation than the glass itself.

Having mixed his ingredients together into the required recipe, or *batch*, the technologist's task is over. When the molten metal emerges from the furnace it is the skill of the glass-blower which takes over. By dipping a blow-rod into the molten metal and swirling it gently, the glass-blower collects a blob or *gather* of glass at the end of the rod in much the same way as he would treacle on a spoon. If required, the gather can be rolled backwards and forwards across a special smooth table called a *marver* to form a rough cylindrical shape which can then be blown to make it hollow. The force of gravity can be used to form the neck of the decanter by swinging the gather until it begins to elongate into a tear-shape. Up until the eighteenth century it was common practice to attach a solid 'pontil' rod to the base of the decanter so that the body would be manipulated and controlled. Once the

decanter had been formed it could be 'cracked off' the blow-rod and held, while still on the pontil, in a small furnace known as *the glory-hole* so that the neck could be reheated and finished off.

Once the neck had been completed, the decanter would then be cracked off the pontil leaving a rough circular mark on the base which would later have to be ground flat.

Although not readily visible, the decanter at this stage of its manufacture is very unstable. Certain parts of the body will have cooled down considerably, while others are still extremely hot. Unless the piece is reheated to a uniform temperature and then allowed to cool slowly, the stress within the metal could lead to fracturing. This final process, known as *annealing* is a most delicate process. Until the development of better heating chambers, known as *leers*, in the mid-eighteenth century up to half the vessels made were broken during annealing.

The vocabulary of façon de Venise

From Medieval times the decoration most favoured on early decanters and jugs was created by the hypoplastic manipulation of the glass while still in its molten state. The Murano workers had been the first to make wide use of the technique and the many European versions, be they in *verre de fougère* or *Waldglas* are generically known to collectors as *façon de Venise* glass. Where it was the actual body of the

24 *Kuttrolf and Ziratflaske.*

decanter which was manipulated, a variety of designs could be achieved; various gadrooned ribbing and fluting could be pincered vertically upwards from the base or *wrythen* to form spiral or swirling vertical reeding. The body could be teased and pulled to make wave-like diamond shapes, and stopper and footrim could be given a wide range of pinched and tooled decoration.

Once the main body had cooled slightly, additional ornament could be created by the application of further areas of molten glass. A wide variety of applied ornament had soon evolved. There was a chain effect achieved by draping loops of glass around the body – a particularly effective ornament on or near the shoulder; blobs, or *prunts* of glass could be added to the bulbous body of the decanter and then impressed with relief lion's heads masks, or strawberry and raspberry patterns; a variety of arches, bands and loops could be trailed in symmetrical patterns down the body; crimped or wavy trails could be draped around the neck to serve the down-to-earth function of a collar to catch any drips of wine which might form after pouring; thicker strands of metal could be draped down the body in vertical lines and further impressed with a wheel to form the *rigaree* pattern of vertical notches; trails of thicker glass could be draped down the body and pincered into repetitive wing-like shapes in the *nipt-diamond-waies* motif (*cf* TYPE 17b); and finally, repetitive trails of interlocking threads could be used to form a chain-like pattern, known as *'guilloche'* which creates a loose looped motif of pincered chain-trailing.

Handles were basically swan-shaped stretching from shortly below the rim on the neck to the curve of the shoulder, where the end of the handle would be folded over (or alternatively sealed with an impressed print), to avoid leaving an unsightly jagged edge. Even though of uniform shape, decoration of these handles was varied. In some instances a thumb-hold would be considerately shaped out of the glass at the top of the handle to give ease of pouring; the handle could be either wrythen to give a barley sugar twist (TYPE 19h) or tooled into a series of bulbous nodules to make the decanter more easily controllable when full.

This type of *façon de Venise* decoration was widely in use throughout Europe. Early versions include a second to third century AD conical 18e ewer with trailed decoration and medusa mask prunt from the Amiens region. From this period up until the sixteenth century and beyond, come

25 An excellent example of the early twisted Kuttrolf style of decanter dating from the seventeenth century. (Victoria and Albert Museum).

also the Venetian and early Germanic pilgrim flasks where the applied glass was frequently of contrasting colours. Venice itself produced numerous sixteenth-century examples of the ewer decanter (TYPE 16a) which was widely imitated in France and the Low Countries. In the German and Bohemian areas early *kuttrolfs* often sported the pincered diamond pattern on their bulbous bodies, and certainly the whole range of *façon de Venise* ornament appeared on the various decanters of the Ravenscroft period in England. In the Low Countries and Holland where the shaft-and-globe TYPE 17a shapes were equally popular throughout the seventeenth century, the nipt-diamond-waies was a popular form of wrythen decoration, while on the later TYPE 17d flagon decanter the body was frequently draped with five or six nipped and pinched vertical trails.

In England, the taste for *façon de Venise* had disappeared by the early eighteenth century, but elsewhere in northern Europe the tradition was maintained, the early nineteenth century being a period when the *Ziratflaske* was at the height of its popularity, its bulbous body a mass of trailed ornament and impressed prunts.

Developments in America from 1780

Only slightly earlier, the first American glass-makers had begun to turn their attention to decorating their wares with applied ornament. When Caspar Wistar's glasshouse in Southern New Jersey was sold in 1780, his former employees spread the knowledge of glass-making outwards from Allowaystown like ripples on a pool and gave rise to the style commonly known today among collectors as the 'South Jersey tradition'. Essentially, this relied heavily on Venetian ornament. Bottles and jugs were either partly blown and then quickly redipped into the molten glass to give a partial decorative layer to the bottom of the vessel, or they were decorated with blobs, prunts

26 *A decanter from 1813—30 period showing early chain decoration and possibly made by Thomas Cains at either his South Boston Flint Glass Works or his Phoenix Glass Works. (Corning Museum of Glass, Corning, New York).*

and trails of molten glass, often in clear contrasting colours. In either case the additional gathers of molten glass would seldom be left untreated, but would be nipped, pulled or tooled to form definite motifs and patterns.

The decanter in Fig. 26 is an excellent example of this 'South Jersey Tradition' decorative technique. It is attributed to one of Thomas Cains' glass-works either in South Boston or Phoenix and dates from the 1813–30 period, a tribute to the fact that the South Jersey tradition extended well into the nineteenth century. The chain decoration around the waist of the decanter is typical, the parallel threads of glass being trailed around the body of the decanter and then nipped together to form the chain, or *guilloche* pattern.

A decorative technique unique to America and the South Jersey Tradition is the 'Lily Pad' motif, used to decorate the lower part of the body of vessels. It was formed by dipping the partly-blown piece back into the molten glass and then pulling glass from the new layer up the body to form stems of glass which terminated in pad-like blobs. Hence the name of lily pad for this type of ware. In the early days it was a very popular form of decoration on bottle-jugs, if not on decanters.

In contrast to Wistar's heavy hard-wearing glass, the wares produced by the next American glass pioneer, Henry Stiegel, were light and delicate and based on the later European styles. But in one particular style of decanter-bottle, he returned to the fluid Venetian lines in a delicate spiralling fluted design. It was created by blowing the decanter into the type of mould used by English and Irish glass-blowers to create the vertical fluting around the base of their decanters. Stiegel, however, extended it right up the body to the shoulder or the lowest neck ring, an effect achieved by blowing the decanter into a part-sized mould to give it the initial ribbed outline and then removing it to finish the blowing. The result was a beautifully soft fluted

ornament which could be either wrythen by twisting it slightly in the final blow or converted into a rough diamond pattern with the use of *pucellas*.

The Nineteenth-century interpretation

The Venetian style of glass-making did not return to England until the mid-nineteenth century when there was a strong reaction to the over-ornate Anglo-Irish wares. To quote the famous art critic John Ruskin in his book *The Stones of Venice* published in 1853 'all cut glass is barbarous: for the cutting conceals its ductility and confuses it with crystal (rock crystals). Also, all very neat, finished, and perfect form in glass is barbarous: for this fails in proclaiming another of its great virtues; namely the ease with which its light substance can be moulded or blown into any form, so long as perfect accuracy be not required'. Instead Ruskin advocated, 'no delicate outlines are to be attempted, but only such fantastic and fickle grace as the workman can conceive and execute on the instant. The more wild, extravagant, and grotesque in their gracefulness the forms are, the better'.

Ruskin's pronouncements were further

27 Two pairs of seventeenth-century style carafes with folded rims and looped handles, standing on short stems with applied beading. Sold for a total of £72 at King and Chasemore.

28 The swirling grace of façon de Venise decoration on this Norwegian 'ziratflaske' made at The Gjovik Werk, near Hurdal, c. 1835. (Victoria and Albert Museum).

imprinted on the mind of the public by a series of exhibitions which featured displays of early Venetian glass. These, together with the South Kensington Museum's policy of commissioning fine reproductions of wares from earlier times, led to several glass-houses looking backwards in history for their inspiration. The two pairs of seventeenth-century style carafe-decanters shown in Fig. 27 are an excellent example of the type of highly individual wares produced. The Stourbridge firm of Hodgetts Richardson, for example, produced several decanters which incorporated the solid stoppers, string-rim pan-lip and applied trailing of the Ravenscroft period.

The views expressed in the *Stones of Venice* also struck a chord with the members of the British Arts and Crafts Movement. The cornerstone of their belief was that no article in house or home, however humble, should sacrifice its potential beauty to either functionalism or commercialism. Anything machine-made had lost its soul, only the hand of the true craftsman could breathe life back into articles of everyday life. With this end in view, William Morris,

29 A glass and silver claret jug stamped on the lid 'Designed by Dr. C. Dresser. Christopher Dresser' and registration mark for 26 March, 1879. (Victoria and Albert Museum).

30 A green glass decanter with silver mounts set with mother-of-pearl with the maker's mark of W. Hutton and Sons Ltd. London hallmark 1902–1903. (Victoria and Albert Museum).

the craftsman-designer who spear-headed the movement, commissioned one of the country's top architects, Phillip Webb, to design a set of table glasses which were to be made at the Whitefriars glass-house of Powell and Sons. It was to prove a happy alliance, with Webb, along with T.G. Jackson and other contemporary designers continuing to ply the firm with ideas. James Powell and Sons was in fact to become the only firm to wholeheartedly revive the traditions of hand-blown glass. The emphasis of their decanters was shape, rather than decoration, favourite medium being delicately tinted green glass. These simple shapes remained a popular expression of the British Art Nouveau into the twentieth century, frequently further embellished, from the 1890s onwards with restrained use of silver mounts, as in the illustrated example by W. Hutton and Sons Ltd.

Early Venetian use of coloured glass and its imitators

Before going on to discuss the other European and American interpretations of Art Nouveau it is necessary to step back in time to consider the other main aspect of the *façon de Venise* style – its creative use of coloured glass. There were four distinctive types of coloured metal made from the fourteenth century through to the sixteenth century when production was at its height: *transparent* coloured metals predominantly in green, amber and ruby, with blue and purple later additions; *marbled* opaque glass known in Germany as *schmeltz* which aimed to imitate a wide range of semiprecious stones; *mosaic* glass, which, like the *millefiori* of the paperweights consisted of rods of different colours being fused together to form a single multicoloured pattern; and a variety of different types of *filigree* in which fine threads of translucent or opaque coloured glass were embedded into a clear crystal glass and blown to the required shape. Depending on the

31 A pair of Dutch decanters mounted in silver by Albrecht V. Wingarden (Hague) 1689. (Victoria and Albert Museum).

arrangement of the rods three types of filigree could be created . . . *vetro a retorti,* or lacy patterns, *vetro a fili* or spiralling and looped threads, and *vetro a reticello*, or criss-crossed threads.

As each new variety of glass appeared on the market it was quickly imitated by the rest of the European glass-world. In the British Museum, for example, there is an early Northern Europe bulbous-bodied jug, made of glass featuring typically Venetian broad bands of opaque white glass alternating with narrow bands of clear glass, the whole mounted with silver-gilt, hall-marked London 1548–9. In Germany, the early form of *kuttrolf* was frequently found with rounded body and pouring tubes fashioned from ornate filigree glass, and in France rare examples of the ewer-decanter (TYPE 16a) have been found in opaque marbled glass with spout, handle and applied prunts in contrasting transparent coloured glass. In many instances it is only the chemical analysis of the glass which reveals that the wares were not actually made in Murano.

Although initially the rest of Europe imitated, it was not long before they also began to innovate. The palette of colours grew slowly. In Germany and France the natural impurities of *Waldglas* and *verre de fougère* leant the metal towards a variety of greens. In Britain and the Low Countries brown, as well as green, was the popular colour for early bottles. By the Ravenscroft period amethyst had arrived, but it was in Bohemia and Germany that much of the early chemical experimentation bore fruit. Early fugitives from Venice may have carried the secret formulae for turquoise brilliant green and blue glass to Hall-in-Tyrol (present-day Austria) during the first half of the sixteenth century but Potsdam in northern Germany was to prove to be the centre from which a whole new range of colours were to appear. Johann Kunckel (*v* 1630–1703) was the famous chemist, who worked there as Director of the Potsdam Factory, and first developed the famous ruby glass around 1679. Other colours attributed to him include blue, green and imitation agate.

Blue and green were to become the favourite colours for the famous tapered and Prussian decanters made in the Bristol area of England during the second half of the eighteenth century. The finest source of cobalt needed to make brilliant blue glass was to be found in Saxony, but there it was jealously guarded for use in the Meissen porcelain factory. The German monopoly was maintained until Dresden fell to the English, during the Seven Years War of 1756–1763, and cobalt could at last be shipped to England. Bristol was the port at which large cargoes

of Saxon cobalt were landed, with the result that all brilliant blue eighteenth-century glass, whether made at the Bristol glass-houses or not, has to come to be known by the generic term of 'Bristol Blue'. The Blue glass was ,the first pride of the Bristol of glass-houses, green glass, also rich and glowing, followed soon after and then the rarer amethyst glass. All were extremely popular until well into the Regency period. The other main *façon de Venise* style of coloured-glass in Britain took the form of

32 Excellent example of the German red glass: a late seventeenth-century/early eighteenth-century example attributed to Kunckel at Potsdam. (Victoria and Albert Museum).

mosaic and *vetro a fili* forms of decoration, both the result of an attempt to cater for the cheaper end of the market. Nailsea, in England was the more important centre, with the Scottish glass-house in Alloa producing much the same sort of wares.

By 1820 the Glass Tax had reached the high figure of 10½d per pound. The excise men were so keen to trap tax-evaders that special sentry boxes had been made at most of the large glass-houses, from which a constant watch could be kept. The one hole in the barrier of red-tape which surrounded the industry lay in the fact that the Glass Tax did not apply so heavily to unrefined bottle glass, and it was this metal which was chosen by the Nailsea glass-makers. From it they made a wide range of decorative peasant-style vari-coloured glasses combined together in a variety of splashed, spattered and striped forms of decoration. Initially the traditional cylindrical bottle decanter seemed most appropriate to the cottage table. But towards the middle of the nineteenth-century Nailsea was producing a more complicated type of coloured glass in which opaque white and pink were merged attractively together to produce more ornamental shapes.

The spattered wares had a definite folk-simplicity about them, but by the 1860s the Nailsea craftsmen were creating more sophisticated carafes, bottles and decanters in swirling loops of *vetro a fili*, using threads of red or blue glass, sometimes both, within colourless glass, their own particular version of the *façon de Venise* tradition being the blowing of spattered translucent mosaic glass in a colourless metal. Similar wares appeared elsewhere in Europe around the same time. An 1850s shaft-and-globe of blue and white filigree spirals made by Belgian workers at Nuutajarvii is to be found in the Finland Glassmuseum, while at the other end of Europe is to be found an 1840s Venetian version of blue and red glass within clear.

In America, it was Wistar who first introduced the New World to a variety of col-

33 A fine example of Catalan façon de Venise glass: the green metal decorated with opaque herringbone motifs, the collar and knop finial in blue glass. (Christie's).

oured *façon de Venise* wares ... pale aquamarines, turquoise, amber, emerald, olive green, brown and opaque white as well as filigrana ... but production was mainly of very simple decanter bottles and decanter jugs. It was not until the Stiegel period that any serious attempts were made to create more ornate decanters in close imitation of Bristol blue or purple glass, and more rarely amethyst and emerald green, the bodies occasionally fashioned in the Stiegel 'wrythen' twirled shapes.

Later, during the early years of the pressed and blown-three-mould patterned glassware a much wider range of colours developed. At Boston and Sandwich Deming Jarves created a beautiful sapphire blue carrying out further experiments to form a variety of purples, yellows, greens, and blues, which he frequently blended together to form 'Marble' glass in the Venetian mosaic tradition. At the Keene works in New Hampshire amber and olive shades had become a speciality, while the Kent glass-house in Ohio had produced a lovely shade of acquamarine. But it was the New England Glass Company which was to become most famous for its ruby glass which was developed around 1848 using 20 dollar gold pieces to produce a rose red which was of a much deeper colour than the yellowish ruby of the true Bohemian glass. From the 1850s onwards this was the most popular colour in the American market, ranging from pale cranberry pinks to lush deep reds. The depth of red was difficult to control especially in stained cranberry glass, and for this reason the claret (TYPE 19g) would frequently be found decorated with a clear stopper and Venetian rope handle, to avoid the use of varying depths of pink.

The New England Glass Company ruby was only a beginning. In terms of colour the period from the 1880s onwards produced a positive rainbow of different hues as America led the world into the era of the Art Glass which was to be closely matched by the English 'Fancy Glass'.

Art glass

One of the prominent figures behind this new 'Art Glass' was John Locke, already established in England for his work with famous glass companies like Hodgetts, Richardson and Co, and Webb Corbett. His famous copy of the Portland vase had won him a gold medal at the Paris Exposition of 1878, but he did not rest there. Keen to pursue artistic methods and techniques, he left England for America in 1882 and within the first year had been offered a job at the New England Glass Company soon to be re-organized into the Libbey Glass Company. It was there that he began to experiment with methods of producing new types of coloured glass in which one shade merged gradually into another. Within a year of his arrival he had patented his first

34 *An early nineteenth-century Nailsea bottle decanter splashed with colour. (Victoria and Albert Museum).*

Art Glass named 'Amberina' in which clear yellow glass was shaded almost imperceptibly into red. From then on his patents kept flooding in. 'Pomona' followed in 1885, a clear glass featuring colour-stained groups of flowers and fruit set against an etched background, using the cornflower as a favourite motif.

Other leading American glass-companies followed suit, a major stimulus to the Art Glass movement coming in the form of an antique Chinese k'ang Hsi vase, decorated in the 'Peach Bloom' manner of white shading to red which came up for auction in 1886. It hit the headlines in the Press when bids reached the figure of 18,000 dollars, and was mistakenly reported as being a 'Peach Blow' vase. Overnight several glass-houses patented their own versions of 'Peach Blow' – all of which slightly differed in tones, the basic principle of shading from white to red reflected in a myriad of similar wares. The New England Glass Company, Hobbs, Brockunier and Co, Wheeling West Virginia, Sandwich, and the Mount Washington Glass Company all brought out their own versions of 'Peach Blow', while in England, Thomas Webb and Sons issued their own version of the Mount Washington 'Peach Blow' together with 'Burmese' glass, under licence from the American Company.

A whole range of patents followed in America including 'Satin' glass, 'Vasa Murrhina', 'Spangled', 'Overshot', 'Marble' glass and a host of others, many of which were used in the making of mass-produced patterned glass, as well as the hand-blown art glass. Vases and bowls were the favourite vehicles for this type of ware but a variety of decanter shapes and claret jugs were also made. Fig. 35, for example, shows Locke's sketches for a range of decanters in 'Amberina'.

English fancy glass

In England a parallel coloured glass movement was being headed by Harry Powell who looked back to the early Egyptian, Greek and Roman glassware for his inspiration, attempting to reproduce the lightly broken surface of the archeological glass finds by modern methods. Other companies followed in his footsteps. In Scotland, early glass was also the inspiration of the Glasgow firm of James Couper and Son who around 1890, developed a new form of glassware which they called by the name 'Clutha', the ancient term for the River Clyde. The glass was deliberately given a streaky, bubbled appearance, almost like the Ravenscroft 'crisselled' glass, in imitation of the Roman glass as discovered by the archeologists. Indeed, the Stourbridge firm of Thomas Webb who also produced a similar ware, gave theirs the name of 'Old Roman'. The predominant colour favoured in the 'Clutha' type of wares was green in a variety of shades, but blues, browns, and even smoky greys, frequently occur.

Nineteenth-century European innovations

To a certain extent Powell's later work, more than that of Cooper or Webb approximated most of the Art Nouveau glass. Art Nouveau may have had its beginnings in France, but the technology on which it depended had begun back in the first half of the nineteenth century when the Bohemians were at the forefront of creating new coloured metals. Josef Riedel (*fl* 1830–1848) had brought new brilliance to glass with his creation of the fluorescent green *'Annagrün'* and fluorescent yellow *'Annagelb'*, metals created by introducing uranium into the metal, and his fellow countryman, Count Georg Franz von Buquoy had contributed a range of opaque coloured metals imitating Wedgewood's basaltes, including sealing-wax-red in 1803 and black hyalinth in 1817. Their efforts bore fruit in the Bohemian coloured glass which was popular throughout Europe. In France, George Bontemps (1799–1884) was the first to pioneer fine coloured glass at the Choisy-le-Roi factory with the introduction of the Venetian filigree, opal and *millefiori* styles of glass, and while he was Director Jean-Baptiste Toussaint introduced the Bohemian coloured glass to the Baccarat factory during the 1851 to 1858 period. Both craftsmen were the founding fathers of the French decorative tableware

and it was from this European melting pot of coloured glass technology that Emile Gallé, founder of the European Art Nouveau glass movement, drew his inspiration. Born into a glass-blowing family, Gallé travelled a great deal, studying in Germany and France, before finally settling down in his home town of Nancy to dedicate the rest of his life to producing original and artistic glassware. In true Ruskin fashion, he and his followers combined originality of both form and colour in the creation of their individually sculptured pieces.

Gallé's main inspiration came from nature, and animal subjects, two themes which often appeared on his vases. But when it came to decanters he drew on a much wider variety of inspirations. In the Musée de l'Ecole de Nancy examples include a cruciform shape, heavily enammelled in the Gothic style of illuminated manuscripts with a picture of a woman drinking, and another in the shape of a barrel, the hoops and staves clearly cut into the body which bears a cameo decoration in blue glass of stylized branches and fruit.

The movement which Gallé started lasted into the 1920s, with several French glass-craftsmen carrying on his traditions after his death. One among them worthy of mention is René Jules Lalique (1860–1945) who opened his own factory at Combs, near Paris in 1908, after spending several years perfecting his own particular style of Art Nouveau jewellery.

His decanters fall into two distinct categories, those which came *en suite* with matching glasses, and those which were intended as single sculptures. The decanter sets are classically simple, made of clear metal, with no decoration at all apart from a simple motif on the stopper or body which would be echoed on the stems of the otherwise plain drinking glasses. The one-offs on the other hand are all completely individual in shape and style, an excellent example being the decanter *'Masques'*. Also highly collectable were his *Caves à liqueurs* which consisted of a central decanter flanked by two shorter ones, all three linked by a central theme: the God Pan with two Bacchantes, for example illustrated in Fig. 36 on which the main decoration is a group of heads arranged around the shoulder. Other similar decanters feature panels of veiled nudes in high relief.

Tiffany and his followers in America

The influence of the Art Nouveau movement gradually spread from France to reach New York in the 1890s with the work of Louis Comfort Tiffany. Tiffany first opened the doors of his glass-works in 1892, manifesting his admiration for Gallé's work in coloured glass decorated with naturalistic motifs. But in 1889, on a visit to Europe, he saw an exhibition of recently excavated Roman glass all of which had acquired a brilliant iridescence through having been interred for so long. It was this iridescence that fired Tiffany's imagination, and he set about experimenting with glass formulae to try and create a similar effect. The result was a range of lustred glassware showing virtually every peacock hue from iridescent blues and golds to shades of bronze and green.

Despite the fact that the iridescence meant that the contents of his decanters were completely hidden from view, Tiffany made a wide range of decanters. A Tiffany booklet of 1905 shows the 'Flemish' design of waisted shoulder decanters with ball stoppers in a combination of gold and lustres. To quote the booklet, 'This Suite of Glass comprises Liqueur, Claret, Sherry and Champagne Decanters'. The general term that Tiffany chose for describing his new style of glassware was *'Favrile'* a name derived from the old English word *'fabrile'* meaning pertaining to a craft of craftsmen. It was a tribute to the ideals of the Arts and Crafts Movement, but unlike William Morris who intended his designs to be readily available to the masses, Tiffany always aimed for the luxury market, finding his clients among the millionaire class of Vanderbilts, Goulds and Havemeyers.

Soon the less exclusive glass-makers had their eyes on the shimmering coloured iridescent wares, and it was not long before imitations began to flood the market. Victor Durand, a former Tiffany workman left to join the Vineland Glass Works in Vineland New Jersey and marketed his Durand Art Glass from there, while the Quezal Art Glass and Decorating Company founded in 1901 was so successful at imitating Tiffany's iridescent wares that the latter angrily began to introduce new lines to try and retain the originality of his work.

Another major glassworks to open its doors at about the same time was the Steuben glass works founded in 1803 by an English glass-maker by the name of Frederick Carder, who, like John Locke before him, had made a name for himself in England before emigrating to join in the American Art Glass Movement. His Steuben Glass Works, which later merged with the Corning Glass Company in 1918 never really developed a specific style of ware. In imitation of the Tiffany style wares, he introduced his own patent glasses 'Aurene', 'Verre de Soie', 'Cluthra Ivrene', and 'Intarsia'. Aurene was a favourite metal for his decanters, usually executed in the traditional 1870s style in either blue, green or gold colours. While for the the Art Nouveau themes of fruits and flowers, he frequently chose cylindrical decanter jug shapes more in keeping with the upright vases which had been the favourite media for Gallé's glass. Finally he produced a wide variety of cut and engraved decanters (Fig. 37) which varied enormously in size and shape.

European interpretations

From America, Tiffany's iridescent look was also brought to Europe, where it found its greatest expression in the Viennese Secession Movement, especially in the irides-

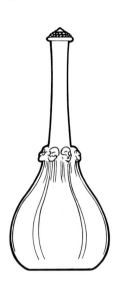

36

38 Typical examples of the late nineteenth-century and early twentieth-century iridescent types of glass. Left to right: a Tiffany favrile bottle and decanter and Bohemian iridescent Lötz decanter.

cent glass, created in flowing *façon de Venise* styles at the factory of Johann Lötz near Klostermüle in Southern Bavaria, which were quickly imitated by other glass-houses in the area.

The glitter and iridescence of the final Art Nouveau phase finally began to fade after the start of World War I, and its place was taken in the 1920s and 1930s by the severe geometric lines of Art Deco. Curved lines were no longer fashionable and the straight line was in. Decanters either cylindrical or conical, and decorated simply with single *façon de Venise* stripes of contrasting colour, either applied as trailing or embedded in the glass.

It is a fitting end to the story of the development of *façon de Venise* to be able to state that from the Art Deco period onwards the mastery of line and colour passed back to its rightful source – the Island of Murano. At the height of the Ruskin revolt in the mid-nineteenth century, reproductions of earlier Venetian styles had been in great demand, yet production on Murano had never been at a lower ebb. Antonio Salviati was one of the first to specifically research into early methods of production and re-educate his workforce at the Salviati works in the arts of the sixteenth-century glass-making. Similar work was produced at the factory of Pietro Bigaglia where production evolved out of techniques learned while repairing examples of antique Venetian glass. By the 1920s the industry was poised to take its newly re-acquired knowledge one step further and create a whole new range of metals which could be used in the *façon de Venise* manner including the sanfirico and filigrane techniques of the elegant Venini decanters.

4   The Art of Enamelling

Façon de Venise glass, with its fluid nipped and trailed decoration, was certainly an ideal medium through which the glass-blower and the chemist could find artistic expression. But the addition of colour to the metal, or the applying of trails and prunts, was not the only way to make glass more decorative. People soon realized that glass could be 'personalized' simply by adding hand-painted motifs to it once the metal had cooled and left the hands of the glass-blower. In some instances the painter or enameller would be part of the team working in the actual glass-house, but as time passed such decorators became 'hausmaler', that is they set up their own studios away from the glass-houses, training their own staff and apprentices to specialize in a particular type of decoration. The advantage of this was that the *hausmaler* could ensure that they always worked on the purest glass, buying their 'blank' decanters from the best available source, and even importing them if necessary.

The process of enamelling is involved, the colours taking the form of metallic oxides suspended in colourless oil. Only when the glass is reheated in a muffle kiln do the colours burst into life, certain colours requiring several firings before they reach their full strength.

Early Venetian enamelling

The Venetians were the early masters of the art, it being a favourite form of decoration for their thin-walled vessels which were too brittle to take the force of the cutting wheel. Few examples of the early thirteenth-century wares have survived, but those from the fifteenth and sixteenth centuries, when a revival of earlier enamelling techniques was led by Anzolo Barovier (*d* 1460)

39 A rare and important pair of Hausmaler spirit decanters by Ignaz Preissler one of which depicts the infant Bacchus, the reverse a scene from the grape harvest, and the other men and women feasting and drinking in a glade c. 1720–1730. Sold for £11,000 at Sotheby's on 5 December, 1977. (Sotheby's).

led frieze of horsemen and ladies and, on the other, women bathing at a fountain of love.

Sapphire blue remained a popular ground colour for Venetian enamelling until the end of the fifteenth century when Murano workers turned their attention to applying enamels to colourless glass. Decorations on pilgrim bottles and ewers now frequently featured the lion of St Mark, or local coats of arms, rather than the more elaborate work of the previous century, a frequent theme around rim and foot being a repetitive pattern composed of gilt or variously-coloured enamel dots.

The art spreads

The art of enamelling spread to the rest of Europe with the first of the glass-makers to escape the prison-like Island of Murano and by the sixteenth century had arrived at Barcelona in Spain and at the Austrian glass-house at Hall-in-Tyrol near Innsbruck. In both instances enamelling took the form of cold-colour decoration, known to the Germans as '*Kaltmalerei*' and to the Venetians as '*dipinto freddo*', in which the decoration was left unfired. In Spain, the sixteenth century enamelled ewers, almost identical to the mid-nineteenth century decanters (TYPE 19i), were frequently decorated with repetitive circling patterns in a variety of yellows, greens and reds as well as enamel and gilt. In Austria, the decoration frequently took the form of floral swans, coats of arms, Tyrolean eagles, wreaths of fruit and abstract Moorish patterns as well as folk-art representations of figures painted in golds reds and blues; a popular shape being the spirit decanter (TYPE 16c).

This square shape, together with the art of enamelling spread gradually northwards through Europe, the cold-colour technique gradually being overtaken by the much more durable conventional muffle-fired enamelling. As late as the eighteenth cen-

40 *A pair of Venetian gilt decanters cut with shallow flutes and decorated with typical Bohemian-style hunting scenes* c. *1775. Sold for £1000 at Sotheby's on 3 May 1976.*

are much more numerous. The Barovier cup in the Murano museum bears witness to the great heights achieved by the Venetians using the traditional Islamic form of enamelling. The cup, made of dark blue glass, has two beautifully painted medallion portraits of the husband and wife for whose wedding it was made, the remainder of the bowl decorated on one side with an enamel-

tury squares (TYPE 16c) were being produced on a large scale in Northern Europe and in Scandinavia, heraldic motifs often replaced by folk figures and simple floral decoration. By the 1770s it was this style that Stiegel had carried to America, his subject matter relying heavily on German folk art motifs ranging from simple floral designs to more ambitious subjects including birds and animals.

The Mid-European contribution

This primitive subject matter, however, did not reflect the heights which German enamelling had reached earlier during the seventeenth century. The new form of enamelling, known as *schwarzlot,* used black enamelling on clear glass to produce finely detailed paintings of religious, allegorical, and historical scenes, in imitation of contemporary oil paintings and prints. Johann Schaper (1621–1670) working in Nuremberg, was one of the early instigators, Daniel Preissler (1636–1733) and his son Ignaz carried the tradition to Silesia, Hermann Benkert (1652–1681) brought it to Frankfurt-am-Main and Johann Anton Carli (*d* 1682) took it to the Rhineland.

Nuremberg, however, remained the most important centre for the development of enamelling, with Schaper joined there by other leading artists like Abraham Helmhack (1654–1724) and Johann Ludwig Faber (fl 1678–1697) who invented some new transparent enamels. At their height the work carried out by these artists equalled the standard of their contemporaries who worked with paint on canvas.

From pure *schwarzlot* they moved to *grisaille*, in which black was supplemented with a range of grey shades to give the subject greater depth. This type of decoration was frequently applied to the early 16c spirit decanters but by the eighteenth century men like Ignaz Preissler were doing a lot of work on shouldered decanter shapes.

The art of enamelling in Britain

Slightly later, the art of enamelling began to flourish in Britain at the hands of William Beilby (1740–1819) and his sister Mary (1749–1797). Their work lasted only a relatively short time from about 1762, just after they had moved to Newcastle-upon-Tyne, until 1778 when they moved to Fife after the death of their mother.

William had received his grounding in painting while working as an artist decorating the then popular enamel boxes in Birmingham. When the family moved to Newcastle, which was well established as one of the finest centres for the production of lead glass, he soon began to earn himself a living by buying plain glass decanters from the

41 *A late eighteenth-century square bottle decanter decorated in cold colour with a picture of a pope or a saint. Height 10½ in. (Victoria and Albert Museum).*

makers and then decorating them with elaborate opaque enamelling.

When he started work his sister Mary was still only in her early teens, but he evidently began to pass his knowledge on to her even at this early age. There is, however, no means of clearly distinguishing the work of brother from sister as all pieces, when signed, simply bear the surname 'Beilby' without mention of Christian names. Only one example of their work has been found with the initial 'W', but in the majority of cases the signature is simply 'V Beilby', 'Beilby inv. & pinx.' or 'Beilby Junr Ncastle Invt. & pinx.'.

Initially, the work featured mainly heraldic motifs and was presumably commissioned to customers' specifications. By the time, however, that his sister had reached the same level of proficiency they were sufficiently well-established to forgo their armorial work. Certainly from the early 1770s their work blossomed into a wide variety of themes from landscapes and conventional floral designs to pure flights of fancy. Particularly sought after by collectors are those pieces which include a butterfly in the design, as this is commonly believed to be a form of Beilby signature. There must have been many other British enamellers working in both coloured and white enamels during the same period as

42 *A heraldic motif typical of the decorative work favoured by William Beilby. (Delomosne and Son).*

43 *The traditional Anglo-Irish shape as employed at the Spanish glassworks at La Granja de San Ildefonso and delicately decorated with enamelling around the shoulder. (Victoria and Albert Museum).*

the Beilbys, but insufficient material has been discovered to give them identities. James Donovan (fl 1770–1829) is the only other artist, working in Dublin, who is known to have enamelled glass as well as pottery and porcelain, but no signed pieces have been found.

44 A range of Bristol glass decanters, the green glass decanters on the right being an unusually fine example by James Giles, c. 1775. Sold for £480 at Sotheby's on 3 October 1977. (Sotheby's).

Gilding on Bristol glass

The Beilby's work was invariably carried out on decanters blown of clear metal but towards the end of the eighteenth century the new brightly coloured Bristol blues and greens began to flood onto the market. Here the rich brilliance of the metal would have outshone any form of enamelled decoration. Instead the ideal companion was gilding.

Apart from the sudden burst of gilding at Murano in the sixteenth century, gilding on a large scale had not been seen since the Islamic period. In the Netherlands, Spain and Hall-in-Tyrol gilding had been used only sparingly to provide gold borders on engraved and enamelled wares. In Britain, it was used extravagantly.

At the lower end of the market more mundane gilding on the Bristol blue and green decanters took the form of the wine label cartouches enclosing the name of the contents, the lozenge stopper also gilded with the initials of the contents, although where examples are found with necks not ground, the most usual accompaniment would have been a cork stopper with silver or porcelain finial.

This type of gilding was well within the reach of semi-skilled gilders, but two Bristol artists were to gain high reputations for much more artistic work involving more elaborate motifs such as are found on the Meissen, Worcester and Sèvres porcelain of the period. Of the two, it was Michael Edkins (1734–1811) whose work is of a slightly earlier date. He favoured the full rococo themes of exotic birds, *chinoiserie*, flowers and insects. Isaac Jacobs (*fl* 1790–1835), coming slightly later was

more influenced by the neo-classic style, frequently decorating the borders of his work with the key-fret motif found on ancient Greek and Roman vases and urns. Outside the Bristol area another well-known independent artist was James Giles (1718–1780) who worked from his London studio on decanter blanks from the Falcon Glassworks and the Parker Glass Manufactory. Pheasants, flowers, and the Meissen-style *fantasie Vögel* were just as popular with him as the more formal neo-classical motifs.

Enamelling on opaque white glass

Coloured decanters in translucent metal were by far the most numerous type produced by the Bristol glass-houses, but they were also well-known for their own version of the opaque white glass which had become popular throughout Europe from the middle of the eighteenth century. The European terms for it, '*porcellana contrafatta*' (counterfeit porcelain) in Italy and '*porceleinglas*' (porcelain glass) in Germany, highlight the fact that it was an attempt by the glass-makers to keep a hold on that side of the decorative glass-market which was gradually being taken from them by the newly-emerging porcelain factories. The decanter illustrated is an excellent example of the rarer Bristol attempts to imitate decorative porcelain (Fig. 44 *centre*).

Elsewhere in Europe similar wares were much more frequently decorated with coloured enamels rather than just black.

Meanwhile in Vienna, a new school of highly pictorial enamelling was being established by Gottlob Samuel Mohn which, carried on by Anton Kothgasser (1769–1851) and Friedrich Egermann (1777–1864) was to sum up the whole spirit of the Biedermeier period, with detailed, almost photographic, enamels of famous buildings, spas, city scenes, and tourist spots as well as portraits and genre scenes. All were aimed at

45 *The beauty of delicate hand-painted enamelling on opaque white glass as executed by the Spanish glass-makers of San Ildefonso.*

the *nouveau riches* who developed an almost insatiable appetite for this type of glass.

The Mary Gregory tradition

While discussing glass from this area, mention must also be made of the Mary Gregory glass, a generic term named after a young artist known to have worked for the Boston and Sandwich Company of America in the 1870s and 1880s, decorating glass in a particular style developed in Bohemia in the mid-nineteenth century. This consisted of white enamel paintings of children executed on coloured glass ranging from the popular rich ruby to green, yellow, amber, amethyst and blue. It was a style which immediately appealed to the Victorian taste; the children, whether catching butterflies, blowing bubbles, tending sheep, climbing trees, or playing games, imbued with that typical romantic innocence which the Victorians always associated with childhood. Highly sought after are matching pairs of decanters in which one decanter portrays a boy and the other a girl so that the two children face each other when the decanters stand side by side. But the greatest rarity of all is the set in which the decanter shows the picture of the leading child while each of the accompanying wine glasses bears a different picture of each of the children following.

Later developments

In England, the 1850s saw a sudden revival of interest in enamelling, following the exhibition in 1847 of 'The Well Spring Carafe'. Made in clear glass by John Fell Christy at the Stangate Glass Works in Lambeth; after a design by Richard Redgrave (1804–1888), in which the main decoration consisted of a series of thin enamelled green leaves extending up the body of the carafe, with a band of flowers

circling the shoulder. The Stourbridge firm of W.H.B and J. Richardson produced many examples based on this same concept, featuring a wide variety of floral motifs from irises to seaweed.

Later in the century it was the French who carried on the enamelling tradition in the work of men like Jules Barbe and Philippe-Joseph Brocard, followed by Emile Gallé who, in the early years of his production, created several decanters of colourless glass which he decorated with ornate Gothic-style enamelling and gilding. However, as Gallé soon realized, enamelling does not really exploit the natural properties of glass – it only serves to mask it. With an improved metal much more exciting results could be obtained by experimenting with etching and engraving.

46 A Mary Gregory decanter with glasses. (Phillips, Son and Neale).

77

5   Engraved and Etched Decanters

Painters and enamellers were not the only ones to be intrigued by the aesthetic possibilities of glass. It offered a whole range of depth and inner light just waiting to be released and potentially it was an ideal medium for the glass-engraver. But it was not until the late fifteenth century that any serious attempts were made to apply the cutting wheel to glass.

The main reason for the delay lay in the very nature of the Venetian *cristallo* glass which was so popular throughout Europe up to that time. Delicate and fragile, it was ideal for draped and trailed decoration, but it was far too brittle for anything more than the lightest of diamond-point engraving. The Crown Heads of Europe, who wanted more brilliant deeply-cut and engraved vessels, had to forsake glass altogether and instead employ lapidaries to carve and cut their jugs and ewers out of rock crystal (the popular term for an extremely translucent type of quartz).

It was exactly these lapidaries, already skilled in engraving rock crystal, who were the first to consider the possibility of transferring their art from semi-precious stones to glass. Despite recent research which shows that it was probably an unknown worker at the Munich court of Duke William V, who first rediscovered the art of glass-engraving as early as the 1580s, it is generally accepted that Caspar Lehmann was the undisputed founding-father of glass-engraving.

Born near Lüneburg in the north of the country, he had arrived in the capital,

Prague, in 1588 at the tender age of eighteen to take up his appointment as court gem-cutter to Emperor Rudolph II. The pieces he worked on were elegant Renaissance vessels fashioned of Bohemian rock crystal, mounted in precious metal and set with precious stones. Exactly when he decided to adapt his lapidary-cutting techniques to the decoration of glass is not exactly known, certainly it must have been around the turn of the century, for by 1609 he had been granted monopoly rights for the production of engraved glass throughout the Emperor's lands.

Technically, Lehmann's major triumph was that he succeeded in carrying out his engravings on the extremely brittle soda glass of the area. It was not until the 1670–1680 period that Bohemian glass-makers discovered that by replacing soda with potash and adding lead they could achieve a much brighter stronger metal. Presumably, therefore, Lehmann's initial attempts took the form of shallow wheel-engraving on fairly thick panels of glass like the 'Perseus and Andromeda' panel attributed to Lehmann which is now in the Victoria and Albert Museum (Fig. 49). But greater than the technical achievement of his work is its artistic brilliance, the fineness

47 *An early Dutch bottle-decanter engraved by Van Heemskerk bearing the inscription* 'Besorg Het Vleesch Niet Tot Lusten' ('*Excite not the desires of the flesh*') *c. 1680. Sold for £8,000 at Christie's on 12 October 1977.*

48 *Wheel-engraving by Anton Wilhelm Maüert of Nuremberg (1672–1737) a mixture of laub-und-bandelwerk and rock work; the reverse engraved with chinoiserie.*

49 *Opposite: The 'Perseus and Andromeda' panel attributed to Lehmann.*

of detail, the subtlety with which he uses the wheel to achieve three-dimensional effects of light and shade. Here indeed was a master of the craft.

The Prague National Gallery has in its collection another of Lehmann's plaques, this time featuring an exquisitely executed bust of Christian 11, the Prince Elector of Saxony. More important, however, they possess one of Lehmann's earliest attempts at engraving hollow ware. That it is by Lehmann is indisputable as it bears his signature 'C Lehmann f 1605'. The picture it portrays is of Liberality, Nobility and Power, after an engraving by Aegidius Sadeler of van der Stratt's painting. The cutting is shallow, but the detail of fruit, flowers, butterflies and beetles is typical of the painstaking care that Lehmann and his followers took.

The influence of wheel-engraving spreads

Of his many pupils George Schwanhardt was chosen by Lehmann to inherit his glass-engraving monopoly. By the time Lehmann died in 1622 Bohemia was already bitterly involved in the Protestant-Catholic struggles of the Thirty Years War. Prague was not the safest of cities in which to remain. On his master's death Schwanhardt returned to his native city of Nuremberg, across the border in the Bavarian region of West Germany, taking with him the vast store of expertise which he had learnt from Lehmann.

The school of engraving which he started, in Bavaria, maintained the high standards which Lehmann had set. Working still on thin-walled locally-blown glass Schwanhardt developed his own particular style of shallow-engraving which incorporated occasional areas of either polishing or diamond-point engraving to give impressions of high relief. In terms of decorative motifs there was a gradual move away from the stylized medieval subject matter of the fifteenth century into the full, flowing

exuberance of the baroque with the vigorous portrayal of mythological and pastoral scenes, frequently enclosed in *laub- und-bandelwerk*.

From the two centres at Nuremberg and Prague, the art of wheel engraving spread rapidly to the east, west and north. Johannes Benedikt Hess brought it west to Frankfurt where the Hesse craftsmen were quick to adopt the Nuremberg style. To the North it travelled through Saxony and Dresden to the Berlin area where Gottfried Gampe and his brothers introduced it at Marienwalden the Brandenburg area. To the north-east it travelled to Silesia (now part of Poland), soon to rival Bohemia with the excellence of its engraving, and to the north-west it travelled through the Thuringian district to the glass-makers of Kassell. While the art of engraving spread and developed, the actual technology of the metal itself hardly changed. It was not until the late seventeenth century that an unknown glass-maker in northern Bohemia first developed a new brilliant metal which could be blown into thicker stronger shapes. Now engravers could apply much deeper cuts to the new bulbous-bodied TYPE 18f decanters – bottles which had just been developed. In Silesia and parts of northern Germany decanter bottles would be decorated with the *hochschnitt*, or cameo-relief technique, the laborious cutting work aided, at the Silesian cutting shop in Petersdorf and the Potsdam workshop in Berlin, by the use of water-power. Elsewhere, in Bohemia and the other German provinces the much easier *tiefshnitt* method of engraving was widely adopted.

The decanter-bottle provided an ideal shape for this much more detailed work. Motifs in the early part of the eighteenth century were still in the highly figurative baroque style, but by the 1760s a much more delicate rococo style had taken its place. In some instances, as in the decanter-bottles produced by Josef Mildner, from the Gutenbrunn in Lower Austria, engraving on the actual glass was

kept to a minimum, and instead medallions featuring scenes engraved in silver or gold leaf set against a red, black, green or blue background would be inset into the main body of the decanter to provide a focal point to the decoration.

The Dutch technique of diamond-point

From the oval Bohemian decanter we move to the flagon decanter (TYPE 17d) which was to be the principle shape for Dutch engraving. The technique of diamond-point engraving, used only sparingly by the Venetians for the occasional restricted embellishment of lips and rims, had gradually spread northwards from Murano through Germany to Holland, where it arrived with

50 Typical inlay work as perfected by Johann Josef Mildner.

full force towards the end of the sixteenth century. At that time engraving suddenly became a popular hobby among the wealthy intelligentsia of Amsterdam and the Hague. Anna Roemers Visscher, a well-known scholar poet, was typical of the many amateurs who produced really fine naturalistic flowers and insect motifs copied from contemporary prints. Her sister Maria was also well-known for her calligraphic work, examples of which are perhaps better known to decanter collectors executed on the popular green-glass flagon decanters of the period by another Dutch engraver Willem Jocobz van Heemskirk.

About the turn of the century diamond-point engraving gradually became much looser in style. Anna Roemers Visscher had begun to incorporate small areas of *stippling* into her predominantly diamond-point work by about 1621, but is was not until a century later, when Ravenscroft had successfully developed his new glass-of-lead that the Dutch began engraving decanter bottles by making use solely of stippling techniques. The glass they worked on was imported directly across the North Sea from the English glassworks at Newcastle, and once engraved much of it, like the illustrated Ravenscroft decanter jug (Fig. 51), returned once more to England decorated by the hands of the Dutch. The most famous of Dutch stipplers were Frans Greenwood, who worked from about 1722 using contemporary mezzotints and prints as the source of his engravings, and his follower, David Wolff, an established painter who, from engravings, from 1770 on, stipple-engraved his own designs and motifs on glass. Wheel-engraving was an art which had to be learnt over a long period of apprenticeship. Diamond-point and stippling, on the other hand, were open to anybody who could handle a sharp engraving tool with the same proficiency as a pen or pencil; hence the large numbers of decanters engraved not just by professional artists, but rather by local outworkers who frequently worked to commission.

51 *A crisselled decanter – jug which is decorated with Dutch wheel engraving, c. 1680–1685.*

Scandinavian interpretations

In Sweden for example the unique conical and pear-shaped decanters were frequently ornamented either with personal inscriptions, framed in trails of leaves and flowers or, more patriotically, with the royal monograms and emblems for sale to all sections of society as well as the nobility; engraving at the Kungsholm Glassworks on similar decanters and carafes, occasionally taking the form of hunting scenes, or, after the arrival of the German engraver Kristoffer Elsterman in the 1690s charming random designs of scattered flowers. Other typically Swedish motifs included the north star and a multi-rayed sun.

In the British Isles the first mention of the art of engraving comes in an announcement made in the Birmingham Gazette of 11 May 1767 (cf F. Buckley *A History of Glass*, 1925) which stated that a forthcoming sale would contain 'The Stock in Trade of a German, who was the first that brought the Art of Cutting and Engraving Glass from Germany. The above named German having met unforseen losses and Misfortunes in the Trade is obliged to sell his Stock for the Benefit of his Creditors.'

The identity of the German is not stated, but Buckley presumes that it could possibly have been the father of Christopher Heady, originator of the 'curious barrel-shape decanter'. Certainly the 'art of engraving' mentioned must have referred to copper-wheel engraving of fruit and vine motifs, for politically-orientated engraved decanters had been known in Britain from a much earlier date.

Jacobite decanters

The period of unrest which they mirror dates from the first part of the eighteenth century when Britain was torn by the same Protestant-Catholic Scottish struggles as had beset Europe during the Thirty Years War. The central theme was the struggle of the Scottish Catholic Pretenders to gain the Protestant English throne. The Jacobites in Scotland who had rallied to the Catholic cause of James II remained faithful to his cause long after he had fled the country in 1688, rising to arms again in the rebellions of 1715 and 1745. After both attempts had failed, open support of the Catholic cause became a treasonable offence, but there was many a household up and down the land where toasts were secretly drunk to the king across the sea, the decanters from which they poured their drinks being symbolically engraved in case they were used as evidence of treason. 'No names, no exile' was the watchword of the day.

In most cases the decoration was of the type shown in Fig. 52 using the White Rose, the emblem of the Jacobite cause, as the main decorative motif.

Other, less obvious symbols include a bird (which stood for the 1715 uprising and the song 'Good luck to my blackbird where'er he may be!'); a thistle (the crown of Scot-

52 A shaft- and-globe decanter.

land); the oak leaf (worn by Charles II when he returned in triumph to London having escaped ten years earlier by hiding in a tree); the grub and butterfly (derived from the old Scots belief that a soul of a patriot buried abroad would always wriggle its way homewards underground to resurface triumphant); and various buds sprouting from the stems of rose or oak springs which symbolized James, Charles Edward, and his brother Henry.

In both England and Scotland, where the Jacobites organized themselves into underground groups, decanters would also sometimes also be engraved with the Society's motto. In the case of the illegal Oak Society the Latin inscriptions *'Redi'* ('return'), *'Redeat'* ('May he return'), or *'Revirescit'* ('He grows strong again'), may be found while their comrades in the Cycle Club favoured *'Fiat'* ('Let it happen').

The greatest boldness of all was to possess a decanter engraved with a portrait of Charles Edward himself framed with the thistle motif together with other Jacobite emblems. Decanters like these, either shaft-and-globe or shouldered, were particularly popular after the disastrous Battle of Culloden in 1746.

Obviously, there was no way in which English engravers would have been responsible for such treasonable engravings, instead it seems most likely that the Jacobites would have bought their decanters from the Newcastle glass-makers and then smuggled them across the sea to Flanders where Flemish engravers would have carried out the work to order. As Charles II had spent part of his exile in Flanders the friendship between the two countries was already well-established.

Williamite decanters

In England it was the Catholics who were in the minority in a predominantly Protestant country. Across the sea in Northern Ireland it was the Protestants who were in the

53 A Williamite claret jug engraved c. 1870 with an equestrian portrait of the King by a Bohemian Hausmaler working in Ireland. Sold for £160 at Sotheby's sale on 25 June 1979.

minority in a predominantly Catholic country. As in mainland Britain, feelings ran high. Things in Ireland had come to a head in 1689 when the Catholic Irish leader Tyrconnel rose against King William in support of James II. In response, some 30,000 Protestants banded together and took refuge in Londonderry, openly declaring their allegiance to William. They remained besieged until William landed at Carrickfergus in 1690 and came to their rescue. The two monarchs, King William and ex-King James, met face to face at the Battle of the Boyne when James and his supporters were routed and the Protestants won the day. Despite their victory, the Protestants who remained in Ireland were still severely outnumbered by Catholics. To keep their spirits up they banded into 'lodges', their proud toast 'to the Glorious and Immortal Memory of King William' or simply 'The Glorious Memory' being a frequent engraved inscription on the decanters produced in large numbers in 1740 to mark the fiftieth anniversary of the Battle of the Boyne.

Typical of these engraved Williamite decanters are the mallet decanter, bearing an engraving of William on horseback, to be found in the Museum of Art in Philadelphia, and a later Prussian decanter, again with an equestrian King William and the inscription 'The Glorious and Immortal Memory of William III', 'Our true Deliverer' to be found in the Ulster Museum. Protestant insecurity was further heightened from the 1760s onwards, when more and more English troops were withdrawn from Ireland to fight the French and maintain control of the American colonies. Not only was there a continued Catholic threat but their land and possessions were constantly under attack from a succession of French, Scots and American privateers who saw the absence of the English army as an excellent opportunity to loot and pillage along the Irish coast. In an attempt to defend themselves the Protestants banded together to form peace-keeping forces and

decanters like the one illustrated to the left and right of Fig. 54 were made at the height of the Volunteer movement in the 1780s. Now to be seen in the Victoria and Albert Museum collection, it toasts the success of the Waterford Volunteers and bears the date of 1782, a year in which several of the Volunteer movements were successful in persuading Parliament to amend some of the more unjust Irish laws.

Another popular portrait figure of the period was Frederick the Great of Prussia (1740–1786) who allied himself with England during the Seven Years War of 1756–1763. Later in the century Horatio, Lord Nelson (1758–1805), together with his famous ship 'The Victory' was another obvious candidate for commemorative decanters.

But not all commemorative eighteenth-century decanters are of such a belligerent nature. It was also a period in which all sorts of different factions within the community were joining together to form clubs and societies. Farmers, for example, were particularly fond of the 'Speed the Plough' motif an example of which is to be found on an Alloa decanter bottle from the Smith's Institute in Stirling, the neck of the decanter engraved with the symbol of crossed forks surmounted by a wheatsheaf. Another popular group were the Freemasons, first formed in 1717, who, by 1800 had lodges throughout Europe, America and Canada. Their emblem appeared engraved on many a decanter on both sides of the Atlantic.

Engraved label-decanters

Commemorative decanters such as those mentioned above, were undoubtedly the earliest to bear engraved decoration. Running side by side with them, however, from the mid-eighteenth century onwards, was the vogue for what have since become known as engraved 'Label-decanters'. The earliest record of their being offered for

sale appeared in the Norwich Mercury in 1755 when a Norwich dealer, by the name of Jonas Phillips announced that he was selling 'New fashioned decanters with inscriptions engraven on them, Port, Claret, Mountain, etc., etc., decorated with vine leaves, grapes, etc.' Prior to this time the contents of one decanter was distinguished from its fellows by a silver or porcelain, 'bottle ticket' which was suspended around the neck of the decanter on a small chain. All that Phillips had done was to transpose the bottle ticket into engraved form. Despite the fact that engraving these labels severely restricted use, label decanters remained extremely popular over the next twenty years and were still being made in smaller quantities long after that date, at least sixteen different names being known to collectors including mountain, spruce, and champain (a form of red wine).

The simplest versions were just decorated on one side, the traditional shallow-

54 On the outside a pair of decanters engraved with the Irish harp and the words 'Success to the Waterford Volunteers 1782' while in the centre is a single decanter engraved with the American eagle and the word 'Liberty'. English, late eighteenth century. (Victoria and Albert Museum).

engraved motifs around the decanter body being that of barley stalks and hop flowers on ale decanters, or the fruiting vine motif of grapes and vine leaves if the decanter has labelled for plain or fortified wines. More decorative and expensive label decanters might feature coats of arms or floral designs engraved on the reverse of the body to the labelled cartouche.

55 Three bell-shaped decanters.

These label decanters are highly popular among collectors, and frequently form the theme for a collection, the aim being to collect as many of the different labels and shapes as possible.

The neo-classical look

But not all engraving took the form of labelled motifs. The new shouldered shapes leant themselves more to all-over engraving. From the 1760s onwards a wide variety of engraved themes, usually polished and resembling light cutting, were used to great effect. It was a period of rococo ebullience and deeper engravings, more in the Bohemian style, were in vogue, with elaborate floral motifs being high in the popularity stakes. Side by side with rococo the neo-classical style was also coming to the fore. In 1768, a publication of Sir William Hamilton's Collection of Greek vases changed the climate of taste. By 1775 rococo styles were definitely on the wane and, with the appearance of the tapered decanter, there was a general swing towards classical elegance, in the form of restrained engraving. Simplicity, in the true Adam style, ruled the roost with decoration restricted to drapes, stars and festoons executed in extremely fine diamond-point and line engraving.

The neo-classical movement had affected most of Europe by this time, and the simple elegance of the English tapered shapes together with engraved motifs were widely imitated. The Bonhomme glass factory at Liège in Belgium favoured drapes and festoons; the St Petersburg Imperial factory sported engraved Imperial eagles and monograms; the Baccarat factory in France combined engraving with gilding; at the Lauensteiner Hütte glassworks in Hanover imitations of the English style bordered on reproduction; in Sweden the fine diamond-point drapes began to appear early in the 1760s running concurrently with the same tapered shape engraved with hunting scenes and in Bohemia the tapered decanter combined engraved monograms with surrounding areas of diamond cutting.

Fire-gilt engraving

The English neo-classical look even extended as far south as Spain. There the traditional shape at La Granja de San Ildefonso was the decanter jug (TYPE 18g) which at first had been afforded the shallow prunty style of Bohemian engraving, much of which was probably executed by Laurence Eder, son of the Swedish master craftsman, who had been brought to Spain in the 1750s. Shortly afterwards Sigismund Brun arrived at the factory from Hanover. Decoration veered towards the northern Bohemian style of wheel-engraving frequently depicting either hunting scenes or gypsy-style full-blown flowers. Brun's unique contribution to Spanish glass was the practice of painting the engraving with a mixture of ground gold-leaf and honey before re-firing the glass in a muffle. The resultant fire-gilding adhered to the areas of engraving making them stand out boldly against the clear glass body of the decanter. This was a uniquely Spanish and Mexican form of decoration, the only similar type of work being that by August Otto Ernst vondem Busch (1704–1779), a German engraver, who stained his diamond-point engravings of flowers and pastoral scenes with black pigment in imitation of contemporary engravings and prints.

56 *Three pairs of decanters showing typical types of decoration current toward the end of the eighteenth century (Delomosne and Sons).*

57 On the outside a pair of decanter bottles wheel-engraved c. 1700 in the manner of Paulus Eder which sold for £3,200 at Sotheby's on 20 June 1978. The central example, bearing mounts by Georg Daniel Weiss, Nuremberg, c. 1710 is unusual in that no other fire-gilt examples are known outside Spain.

By the late eighteenth century the Spanish fire-gilding was being applied to the tapered English decanter shapes, the engraving floral rather than neo-classical. Such folk-art engraving was also popular in the Scandinavian and northern European glass-houses, especially on square spirit decanters (TYPE 16c) which had come into wide use with the increased popularity of brandy and aquavit during the eigh-

teenth century. Taking this northern European tradition with him, similar floral motifs were among the first engraved on the English Bristol type decanters at the Stiegel works in America.

Early American engraving

As none of Steigel's pieces have been found to bear any identification marks, the attribution of the engraved shoulder decanter in Fig. 59 is tentative, although it is generally assumed to have come from his Mannheim works in Pennsylvania. Where Stiegel favoured more primitive decoration, Amelung, the next important glass-maker in America, concentrated his efforts on producing really excellent, detailed engraved wares. Numerous commemorative and presentation pieces, including the famous tumbler inscribed to his wife with the words 'Happy is he who is blessed with virtuous children. Carolina Lucia Amelung, 1788', have enabled the experts to definitely pin-point Amelung's commemorative wares. For several years though, his Anglo-Irish styles slipped through the collecting net and went unrecognized. Then someone thought of carrying out chemical tests on some supposedly imported Anglo-Irish wares. The formula turned out to be soda-lime, not lead. As soda-lime glass was never used to make eighteenth century decanters in either England or Ireland this proved, without a shadow of a doubt, that they had come from Amelung works. It is testimony to the high quality of the decanters which he produced

that even experts could not tell imported from Colonial.

The reason for this confusion lay in the fact that Amelung decanters imitate so faithfully those made in England, Ireland and the Continent. Mostly he favoured the tapered shape, with comb-fluting around the base, and conventional disc and lozenge-shaped stoppers. Engraved ornament came in two varieties: classically restrained (reminiscent of the French decanters where an engraved band with drapes and festoons of engraved ornament falling from it encircles the waist or shoulder of the decanter) and the folk-art versions with motifs like that of crossed

58 A combination of engraving and the gilding so much favoured by the Spanish factory at San Ildefonso, this example dating from the mid-eighteenth century (Victoria and Albert Museum).

59 A shoulder decanter showing the typical floral motif associated with Stiegel, and possibly from his Manheim glass-house; c.1765–1774. (Corning Museum of Glass, Corning, New York).

barley-ears engraved to denote contents, or with purely fanciful decorations of birds, leaves and foliated sprays.

By the time O'Hara and Craig were pioneering the glass industry in the Pittsburgh area, decanters were following the styles of the Anglo-Irish period with the Prussian making its debut soon after the 1780s. By this time the delicate classical motifs of the Amelung period had been supplanted in popularity by the more traditional fruiting vine. An excellent example of the American Anglo-Irish Prussian is shown in the decanter in Fig. 61 which is attributed to the Charles Ihmsen 'Birmingham Glass Works' in Pittsburgh, Pennysylvania.

Return to Europe

In Britain, as the Anglo-Irish period progressed, the taste was more and more for cut decoration applied to the Prussian shapes, the notable exception being in the Newcastle area, where engraving, under the Dutch influence, was kept very much alive, TYPE 18p frequently being decorated around the shoulder and upper body with fruiting vine motifs, or abstract bands of patterned etching.

Like the tapered shape before it, the Prussian was soon an accepted shape throughout Europe, continuing to be made long after it had fallen out of fashion in England. From the 1840s the Russians for example, produced large quantities, frequently decorated with transfer prints. The process was probably invented in England around 1753, but was not widely in use until the early years of the nineteenth century, designs printed in monochrome on opaque white glass, or occasionally printed in outline and then filled in with polychrome painting. The Birmingham firm of George Bacchus and Sons introduced it about 1809, and other firms, like Henry G. Richardson & Sons are knows to have used it as well.

60 A purple glass decanter cut on the wheel with silvered and gilt decoration which shows the marriage of the Continental Empire taste with that of the Anglo-Irish period, possibly from the St. Petersburg Imperial factory in Russia. (Victoria and Albert Museum, London).

61 Opposite: Engraved with the ships Hornet and Peacock, and with a pressed stopper, this decanter possibly comes from the Birmingham Glass Works of Charles Ihmsen in Pittsburgh, c. 1873. (Corning Museum of Glass, Corning, New York).

Bohemian cased and flashed glass and its imitators

The other style of engraving, running concurrently with that of the Anglo-Irish period was that in early nineteenth century Bohemia. As explained in Chapter 3, the late eighteenth and early nineteenth century found the Bohemian glass-men suddenly producing a whole new range of coloured metals which could be cased onto clear glass. Shallow *wheel-engraved motifs* would then be cut through the coloured layer so that the engravings appeared as clear glass which contrasted with the surrounding coloured background. The most popular decanter shape for this type of ornamentation was the elegant Victorian cylinder (TYPE 19d). In its simplest form the engraved decoration would be of the fruiting vine motif, but more elaborate versions featured a variety of hunting scenes, stylized landscapes, leaf and bird designs, or the Mary Gregory style pictures of children.

Production of this engraved coloured glass, together with the cut-cased glass dealt with in Chapter 6 heralded an unprecendented expansion in the Bohemian glass-industry as the new coloured glass was exported all over the world. The statistics speak for themselves: 25,000 workers employed in the Novy Bor region alone; a total of 169 furnaces in the country as a whole – the 1876–1800 American imports of 'Bohemian cut, engraved, painted, coloured, printed, stained, silvered, or gilded, plain, mold, and pressed glass' totalling $2,972,089.76. So rapid was the expansion of the industry that schools of engraving were set up throughout Bohemia. One of the most famous was that set up in Karlsbad by Andreas Vincenz Peter Mattoni (1779–1864). It produced many important engravers including Ludwig Moser (1883–1916) who did much commissioned work for the Imperial Court and eventually went on to open his own glass-works.

Under such a concentrated attack the rest of the glass-making world adopted the Bohemian style as soon as their own industry had mastered the technique of producing equally brilliant colours, and where possible they employed Bohemian craftsmen.

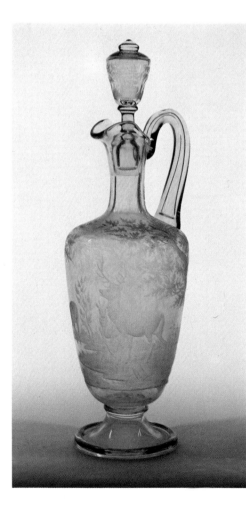

62 Left: A fine example of Bohemian engraving through cased or flashed glass the subject matter typically on forest and hunting themes.

63 Right: A combination of cutting and engraving through opaque white glass to clear which was a more restrained interpretation of the Beidermeier look.

94

The revival of engraving in England began in the 1830s and 40s with Stourbridge glass-makers like the Wood family of Brettell Lane and Thomas Hawkes of Dudley, becoming proficient at engraving ruby-red stained glass. In France, the Baccarat factory was soon in full production, and, in competition with Bohemia, was exporting French Bohemian-style glass to surrounding countries. M. Souzay, writing at the time, claimed that in fact the French imitations were superior to the original Bohemian wares which 'are less finished in detail than ours; the defective objects are put up for same with the others; the mouths of bottles and other like objects made with carelessness which would not be tolerated in France'.

Engraving on colourless glass

The universal revived interest in engraving gradually began to shift from coloured glass to work on colourless metal. At the turn of the century much of this took the form of commemorative wares. As early as 1791 the Amelung works in America had produced a bottle-flask signed 'F. Stanger 1791' and engraved with the Masonic symbol together with a foliate wreath and a plough, and in England the popular Ango-Irish cut decanters were frequently decorated with Masonic emblems. But a new brand of commemorative ware was developing to celebrate the achievements of the new technology

In America, Robert Fulton had invented the first steamship which crossed the Atlantic in 1819, new waterways (like the Erie Canal of 1825), had been opened and the railways were forging new iron roads across the States. In England, the industrial age was also on the move with railway and canal companies all needing their own engraved decanters, while the ordinary householder was still buying glassware to commemorate events like the opening of the Sunderland bridge in 1796. Then, from the 1860s, the

64 The popular fern motif engraved on a claret jug of the late nineteenth century.

emphasis was more on naturalistic subject matter. The standard of engraving became progressively higher and three new types of decanter were introduced specifically with the engraver in mind: the nineteenth-century Victorian claret and the classical shapes (TYPES 19i and 19j).

New standards set

A variety of new engraving techniques were soon revived or developed, but, before dealing with these more exotic fields mention should be made of the more readily available engraved decanters. The early commemorative wares gradually gave way to various wild-flower, exotic or garden floral motifs, most popular of which was the fern motif developed by John Ford while working with the Holyrood glassworks in Scotland. It was first exhibited in 1862 and was immediately widely imitated, especially by the imigrant Bohemian engravers. At the hand of Johan Millar and Emmanuel Lerche it was to continue in popularity until the end of the nineteenth century. The tradition of fine engraving, once established in Scotland, has continued to the present day, important exponents being Colin Terris and Bruce Walker.

John Northwood and cameo techniques

The new experimental school of engraving had been started in England, shortly after the 1851 Exhibition, by John Northwood (1836–1902) who worked first with the firm of W.H., B. & J. Richardson, and later with Stevens & Williams. He was the artist who successfully rediscovered the ancient Roman technique of cameo carving. His first work in this style was a small vase, finished in 1860 which depicted St George and the Dragon cut in cameo relief on an overlay metal. His greatest work, however, was the reproduction of the famous Portland Vase which he finally completed in 1876. The original first century vase had baffled experts since its discovery near Rome in 1582. No-one could be completely sure of what it was made. Via the Duke of Portland it had come into the hands of the British Museum where it was proudly put on show. When, in 1845, it was shattered by a young Irish fanatic, a reward of £1,000 was offered for the first person to produce a convincing replica of it. Wedgwood, who was sure that it was made of pottery or porcelain, made a study of the fragments and as a result produced his famous range of blue and white pottery. Northwood, however, was convinced it had been made of deep blue glass cased with an overlay of opaque white metal which had then been wheel-engraved to produce the cameo effect. It took him six years to produce his replica, but he was right. The vase had been made of glass.

As a result of his work, a school of engraving was established in Stourbridge with other famous cameo engravers including Joseph Locke and the Woodall brothers. The hand-carved cameo technique turned out to be an extremely lengthy process and it was not long before commercial versions were being brought out using the acid cut-back method to remove large areas of background.

Acid cut-back

As early as 1771, a Swedish chemist by the name of Scheele had discovered this highly corrosive effect of certain acid on glass. But it was not until the Northwood era that glass-makers began to put this discovery to creative use. To quote Harry J. Power in his technical work *Principles of Glassmaking* published in 1883, 'etching consists in the corrosion of the surface of glass by hydric fluoride. Patterns are produced by covering the whole surface of the glass with a thin coating of wax, removing the parts to be etched, and plunging the vessel into a solution of acid.' In some cases this sort of treatment would form the initial stages of cameo or intaglio engraving, it being far easier and far quicker for the artist to use the acid to remove the background layers than for a workman to spend laborious hours using the wheel. With this largish proportion of the work done for him, the artist could then afford to spend a greater amount of time on the more intricate work.

The Stourbridge firm of Thomas Webb was by far the most important producer of such more-reasonably priced cameo glass, examples including a square spirit decanter which featured a panel with the word 'whiskey' on it surrounded with a trailery of rose buds and leaves carved out of triple-layered coloured glass. Another Webb decanter in the Carl Pilz Collection features floral intaglio carving on the body.

In France, Gallé also made extensive use of the acid-cutback method for his floral themes and Lalique produced several decanters depicting pastel shade landscapes. Followers included Frederick Carder (1836–1963) at Steuben in America and Simon Gate (1883–1945) who while working at the Orrefors Glasbruk in Sweden produced a new coloured 'graal' glass in which the etched or engraved piece was reheated, to soften the design, and then flashed with clear glass.

Apart from apply etching and engraving to opaque glass the nineteenth-century saw extremely fine work carried out on colourless glass. In Paris, Charpentier (fl 1813–1819) won a high reputation for delicate engraving of goddesses and *amorini*, working on fine lead crystal from the Belgian Vonêche Glassworks. In the Netherlands, Daniel Henriquez de Castro (d 1863) revived interest in early Dutch engraving, especially David Wolf's work and established a style of his own combining stippling and line engraving with etching. Others to follow in his footsteps include L Adams, Andres Melort, E Voet and lately Willem Heesen chief designer at the Royal Dutch Glassworks at Leerdam from 1943.

In England, the main emphasis was on the same kind of delicate extremely fine-lined style of engraving which paid attention to the most minute detail. Frederick Engelbert Kny, a Bohemian engraver, who worked for Thomas Webb & Sons from the 1860s became an undisputed master of *intaglio* work, producing several intricately engraved decanters featuring eastern motifs which were at the height of popularity in the 1880s and 1890s.

Rock crystal engraving

Kny was also a leading name in 'rock-crystal' engraving which was the invention of William Fritsche, a fellow Bohemian working at Webbs. It was based on the same type of lapidary wheel-engraving known to Caspar Lehmann some four centuries earlier, Fritsche's innovation being the use of acid-polishing which on the superior nineteenth-century metal created exactly the same effect as if the engraving had been carried out on natural rock crystal. Both men exhibited their work, to much applause, at the Paris Exhibition of 1878. Fritsche's exhibit took the form of a ewer featuring a deep-cut mask of Neptune below the lip, with fish and wave motifs around the body and a pattern of shells to ornament the foot. Kny's contribution was equally classical in inspiration: a claret decanter engraved with a relief frieze adapted from the equestrian section of the Parthenon brought back with the Elgin Marbles. Joseph Keller at Stevens and Williams and F Eisert, were but a few of the many other British artists who tried their hands at this particular type of engraving.

65 The Elgin claret jug engraved on the wheel by F.E. Kny for the Paris Exhibition of 1878, while he was working at the Thomas Webb's Dennis Glasshouse in Stourbridge.

In the 1880s and 1890s these various types of engraving were equally popular on both sides of the Atlantic. In America it was the N.E.G.C. who spearheaded the new artistry, employing engravers like Louis F Vaupel, Leighton, and Fillebrown, Vaupel's engraving being so detailed that he even managed to portray the muscles on the animals he engraved. Other firms soon followed N.E.G.C.'s lead, an excellent example being the pair of decanters in Fig. 67 while in the twentieth century the Hungarian-born Joseph Libisch won world-wide recognition for the work he did at Steuben under Frederick Carder (1836–1963) implementing ideas by famous designers like Sidney Waugh.

The twentieth century has witnessed continued interest in really top quality engraved glass ever since. Steuben has continued to be at the forefront of work in America, Simon Gate and Edward Hald have established Orrefors in Sweden as one of the leading engraving schools in Europe and in Germany by Wilhelm von Eiff has

revived the 'hochschnitt' technique.

As far as collectors are concerned, however, by far the most detailed and artistic work in this country has been by Laurence Whistler and his followers, Whistler's favourite shape being the traditional three-ringed Prussian decanter with target stopper.

66 *Opposite: A magnum claret decanter of crystal glass, one side depicting a view of Alexander Palace, the other bearing an inscription to Sir Silb John Gibbons, Lord Mayor of London 1872 and signed 'Eng. by F. Eisert', c. 1872.*

67 *A pair of decanter-bottles with stoppers, cut and engraved with galloping horse and hounds and initial 'R' cut by J. Hoare and Co. (Corning Glass Museum, Corning, New York).*

68 The expert hand of William Fritsche engraved this decanter in 1890 while he was working for the Webb glasshouse in Stourbridge. Sold for £260 at Christie's.

A glossary of terms

ACID ENGRAVING

Hydrofluoric acid is used to attack areas of glass not protected by resists like wax, gum or varnish. If acid is used on its own, the etching will be clear and bright, if mixed with a neutralizing agent, such as ammonia, the result will be frosted or white satin. Numerous effects can be achieved by varying the concentration.

ACID CUTBACK

Acid is used to bite through an outer layer of cased glass to reveal contrasting coloured layers beneath.

ACID POLISHING

Once engraved the piece is dipped in a solution of hydrofluoric and sulphuric acids, which polish the engraved areas not covered with resist.

CALLIGRAPHY

Inscriptions diamond-point engraved in extremely elegant, flowing, decorative script.

CAMEO GLASS

Engraving on cased glass using a process in which large areas of the surface are cut away leaving the design standing in high relief against a background of glass in a contrasting colour.

CASED GLASS

A gather of glass is blown into a mould with subsequent second and even third gathers of glass in contrasting colours additionally blown into the same mould. Removed from the mould the piece is then heated to fuse the various colours into one solid body of glass composed of different layers which could then be engraved in the *cameo* technique

COLOUR ETCHING

Designs are scratched onto the surface of the glass using a suitably sharp instrument fitted with a diamond or flint tip.

DIAMOND BURR ENGRAVING

A modern form of diamond-point using an implement rather like a dentist's drill to produce engravings composed of rough-edged lines of trailed dots.

ETCHING

Acid engraving using a very fine instrument to scratch away the resist as opposed to using the wheel. The distinctive feature is that there is no tangeable roughening of the surface.

FLASHED GLASS

A gather of clear uncoloured glass is dipped into clear coloured glass before being blown into the required decanter shape, the engraving cut through to the colourless glass.

HOCHSCHNITT

The form of relief engraving in which the wheel is used to remove background areas of the glass leaving the main motifs standing proud from the rest of the surface.

INTAGLIO ENGRAVING

The reverse of *Hochschnitt*, the engraved design biting through the outer layer and appearing beneath surface level.

LAUB- UND BANDELWERK

Baroque engraving involving strapwork and interlacing leaf motifs, occasionally with additional scenes in the style of chinoiserie. Widely used in Nuremberg, Bohemia and Silesia.

MATTSCHNITT

The engraved motif was not polished but left matt so that it would appear in clear contrast to the background of polished glass.

ROCK CRYSTAL ENGRAVING

Wheel-engraved work carried out in the 1880s and 1890s in which the engraving with acid-polished.

SAND-BLASTING

Glass is bombarded with a high-pressure spray of sand, flint or similarly hard material, the speed of the spray adjusted to give a variety of depths and degrees of matt finish.

SATIN GLASS

The opposite of etched glass, the acid being used as an acid cut-back to remove the surface from around the protected design which remains polished.

STIPPLED ENGRAVING

The design made by striking the glass with various hard-pointed instruments to build up a picture composed of tiny dots, as opposed to scratched lines.

TIEFSCHNITT

Really deep *intaglio* decoration.

VETRO CORROSO

A modern form of acid engraving in which the resist resin crackles on drying so that when treated with hydrofluoric acid the result looks like crackled ice.

WHEEL-ENGRAVING

The wheel is used in glass decoration for both cutting and engraving but there are four main differences between the two techniques. (1) In cutting the wheels are usually made of stone, while in engraving they are of copper or bronze. The notable exception to this rule being in America where stone wheels were occasionally used for engraving as well. (2) The diameter of the wheels used for engraving is much smaller, varying from four inches down to the size of a pin head. (3) The engraver holds the glass underneath the wheel to apply the decoration, while in cutting the glass is held above the wheel. (4) In the early days the lathe for engraving was powered by a foot treadle under the direct control of the engraver, while for cut glass the wheel was turned by an assistant.

Famous exponents

DOMINIK BIEMANN (1800–1857) Prague and western Bohemian spas: engraved portraits and landscapes.

JACOBUS VAN DEN BLIJK (1736–1814) Dutch: stippling famous paintings.

AUGUST BOHM (1812–1890) Bohemian: Biedermeier figure subjects.

ELIZABETH CRAMA (fl *c* 1677–1698) Dutch: diamond-point and calligraphy.

CASPAR CREUTZBURG (fl *c* 1689) Thuringian wheel-engraver, combined pictorial work with lengthy inscriptions.

ERHARD DORSCH (1649–1712) and his son CHRISTOPH DORSCH (1676–1732) Nuremberg.

JOSEF DRAHONOVSKY (*b.* 1877) Czech glass-engraver designing in classical mode.

PAULUS EDER (fl 1685–1709) Nuremberg: fine detail, *tiefschnitt* wheel-engraving.

GOTTFRIED GAMPE (fl 1668) Bohemian engraver, brought wheel-engraving to Brandenburg in Germany.

FRANZ GONDELACH (1663–1726) From 1688 at Hesse-Cassel: baroque, pastoral, allegorical, biblical in *hochschnitt* or *intaglio*.

FRANZ GOTTSTEIN (fl 1810–30) Leading Austrian engraver, first in Moravia, then Gutenbrunn.

CHARLES GRAFFART(1893–1967) Modern Belgian designer and wheel-engraver at Val-Saint-Lambert.

FRANS GREENWOOD (1680–1761) Rotterdam: stippled engravings after contemporary prints and mezzotints.

EDWIN GRICE (1839–1913) Worked with John Northwood on cameo engravings.

WILLEM JOCOBZ VAN HEEMSKERK (1613–1692) Amateur Dutch diamond-point; calligraphy.

G H HOOLART (fl 1770–1780) Dutch: stipple-engravings.

HEINRICH JÄGER (fl 1690–1720) A Bohemian, brought *tiefschnitt* engraving to Berlin: designs depicting the human figure.

JOHANN CHRISTOPH KIESSLING (fl 1717–1744) Saxony, Germany: hunting scenes.

GEORG FRIEDRICH KILLINGER (fl 1694–1726) Nuremberg: combination of diamond-point and wheel engraving, but later deeper wheel-engraving.

HEINRICH GOTTLIEB KÖHLER (fl 1746–1781) Silesian: landscapes at Copenhagen and Nöstetangen.

GEORG ERNST KUNCKEL (1692–1750) Gotha, Thuringia: intaglio engraving using pearl festoons and trellised lambrequins.

PAUL MICHOT: director at the Baccarat factory, introduced wheel-engraving between 1867 and 1883.

ANTON WILHELM MÄUERL (1672–1737). Nuremberg engraver: interlaced foliage of *laub- und bandelwerk*.

FRANZ JOSEPH PALME Bohemian engraver working for Thomas Webb and Son from the 1880s: engraving animals.

KAREL PFOHL (1826–1894) Steinschönau *hochschnitt*: horses on cased or flashed glass.

JACOB SANG (d 1783) Dutch: commemorative and heraldic motifs.

HANS WOLFGANG SCHMIDT (fl 1676–1710) Nuremberg: battles, ruins, hunting scenes.

CHRISTIAN GOTTFREID SCHNEIDER (1710–1773) Silesia: combination *hochschnitt* and *intaglio* engraving: detailed pastorals and allegorical motifs based on contemporary Augsburg prints.

AERT SCHOUMANN (1710–1792) Dutch stipple-engraver.

A F à SCHURMANN (1730–83) Amsterdam stippling with hatching.

GEORG SCHWANHARDT THE ELDER (1601–1667) Nuremberg: landscapes and baroque scrollwork, some acid polished.

HERMANN SCHWINGER (1640–1683) Nuremberg: views of famous buildings, bacchanalian scenes, calligraphic inscriptions, pastoral landscapes.

GOTTFRIED SPILLER (c 1663–1728) Silesian at Potsdam, *tiefschnitt* and *hochschnitt*, mythological scenes, *putti* and figures.

GIACOMO VERZELINI (1522–1616) Venetian: brought to England by Jean Carré in 1571, first to produce diamond-point wares at his factory, probably done by Anthony de Lysle, a French artist-engraver who worked for him.

ANNA ROEMERS VISSCHER (1583–1651) amateur Dutch: calligraphic inscriptions accompanied by flowers, fruit and insects copied from contemporary prints. Her sister Maria: calligraphic engraving.

DAVID WOLFF (1732–1798) Dutch, the Hague, stippling.

GEORGE WOODALL (1850–1925) and THOMAS WOODALL (1849–1926) Cameo engraving for Thomas Webb & Sons, England.

6

The Brilliance of Cut Glass

As we saw in the last chapter, the revival of glass-cutting first began with the lapidary work of the German and Bohemian master craftsmen. They were the first to develop a clear metal which was strong enough to take the full force of the cutting wheel, but the metal itself did not have the same refractive brilliance of the later lead crystal developed in England. As a result the Bohemian glass was a better vehicle for the matt finish of copper-wheel engraving so that deeper cutting and faceting was restricted (on TYPE 18f of decanter bottle) to shallow printies extending up the neck to the rim, or simple lapidary faceting on the spire stoppers.

The Ravenscroft metal was to prove a much better vehicle for the heavier cuts. Unfortunately, at the time of its discovery there were no competent glass cutters in England. That knowledge probably first arrived in England in the wake of George I, Elector of Hanover, who came to the throne in 1714, and probably brought a few master-cutters with him from Germany. Within only a few years John Ackerman, a London maker, known to have employed at least one German cutter, was advertizing in 1719 'all sorts of tea, chinaware, plain and diamond cut flint glasses'. Several other such trade notices from the first half of the eighteenth century also refer to things like 'cut-glass in the current fashion', yet despite this, very few early examples of cut-glass decanters have survived the test of time. The cut decanter in Fig. 70, which dates from about 1750 and is currently in the

Victoria and Albert Museum, is a rarity indeed. In fact, it seems likely that Ackerman was the only one to be seriously experimenting with the novel cutting techniques, for, as F. Buckley points out in his 'History of Old Glass' (1925), an announcement which appeared in the Birmingham Gazette of 11 May 1767, heralded the sale of The Stock in trade of a German, who was the first that brought the Art of Cutting and Engraving Glass from Germany. The above named German having met unforseen losses and Misfortunes in Trade is obliged to sell his Stock for the Benefit of his Creditors'. Buckley presumes that this was the father of Christopher Heady, originator of the 'curious barrel-shaped decanter', and that he may also have been the German cutter employed by John Ackerman in the late 1720s.

Certainly the Glass Excise Act of 1745 would not have helped this unknown German to stay in business. As discussed in Chapter I, the new level of tax precluded the blowing of the thicker-walled decanters which are needed for anything but the shallowest of cuts. From about 1745 to 1755 there prevailed a fashion for cutting decanters all over in a continuous design of shal-

69 *A fine pair of shaft and globe decanters heavy cut in the late Anglo-Irish style c. 1845.*

70 A rare mid-eighteenth century cut-glass decanter with faceted stopper. (Victoria and Albert Museum).

low diamond-shaped facets and then from the 1760s there was a short period when the shaft-and-globe shape became almost smothered with detail, but these vogues were relatively short-lived. Instead the mainstream of decanter taste favoured the more delicate, thin-blown, rococo shouldered and tapered shapes (TYPES 18i and 18 l).

The most uniformly adopted areas for cutting if the decanter was to be engraved, were the neck, the shoulder and the lower part of the body just above the base. Around the base the traditional design was of herring-bone, or comb fluting, which would extend a quarter of the way up the body. Mirroring this would be slightly broader shallow-cut flutes extending down the neck to the shoulder, leaving the centre of the body free for appropriate rococo engraved ornament.

By the 1770s the cutting wheel was becoming more adventurous, the neck being decorated with a continuous pattern of hexagonal or polygonal scale cuts, and the body decorated with deeply cut stars, drapes or festoons.

It was this extremely basic cutting vocabulary which the English craftsmen carried with them when they crossed the Irish Sea in the 1780s, after parliament had decreed that the ban on Irish exports should be lifted.

The Anglo-Irish migration

The extent of the English migration is best illustrated by a report of 1785, given as evidence before a Parliamentary Committee into commercial relations between Great Britain and Ireland. In it a case was cited of 'a Mr. Hill, a great manufacturer of Stourbridge', who 'had lately gone to Waterford and taken with him the best of the workmen he could get (between fifty and seventy) in the county of Worcester'. Migration on such a large scale obviously had a considerable effect on the English

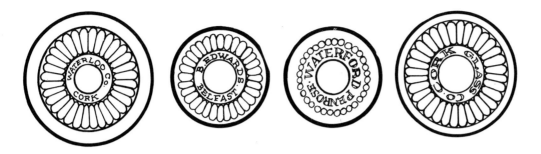

industry, but it would be wrong to imagine that it crippled it completely. Through the Anglo-Irish period, English glass-houses outnumbered the Irish by an average of five to one and there are more than sufficient grounds to believe that large quantities of the English glass were smuggled across the waters to be exported from Ireland as Irish glass. In learning to distinguish the genuine early Irish decanter from its English counterpart, the work of M.S. Dudley Westropp, who wrote the guide for the National Museum of Dublin, is an invaluable source of information. His book *Irish Glass* published in 1920 is still the standard textbook for those who want to make a speciality of collecting Irish glass.

Irish cut glass

It goes without saying that those decanters most easily recognizable are the ones which bear the moulded name of the company on the base. Such trade marks were formed by blowing the glass into a tapered mould which left the circular imprint of the name of the factory on the base, while at the same time forming vertical moulded flutes up the bottom part of the body. Only the bottom section of the decanter would be moulded in this way, using a shallow mould, tapered to the base to make withdrawal of the finished vessel easier.

The four marks of the major companies are illustrated in Fig. 71. Other marks which

occur include those of 'Francis Collins, Dublin' . . . 'Mary Carter & Son, Dublin' . . . and 'Armstrong Ormond Quay' (all of whom were probably glass dealers), as well as "C.M. & Co' which stood for the Dublin glasshouse of Charles Mulvany which opened in 1785, but whose decanters are otherwise indistinguishable from examples made at the other Irish factories.

Which brings us to another point. The major Irish factories did not always make use of the mould to impress their company mark. Many decanters were completely free-blown and bore no mark at all, and it is these examples which are generally considered by collectors to be far superior to their marked contemporaries. When ascribing these unmarked pieces to a particular factory the decanter may provide the clues to identify: the moulded factory marks (Fig. 71), the stoppers (Fig. 72), the neck rings (Fig. 76), the form of decoration (Fig. 75) and the overall shape.

Belfast

The first of the major Irish glass-houses was built in Belfast by Benjamin Edwards in 1776, passing on his death, in 1812, into the hands of his son who continued in business until about 1829. Edward was a Bristol manufacturer and he bought the traditional taper decanter shape with him, giving it a slightly more bulbous waistline than the true slim-lined English tapers. A typical

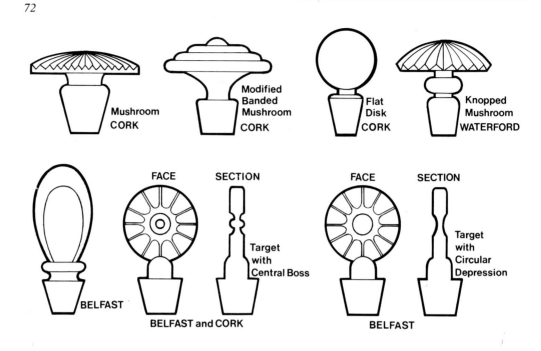

Belfast shape is to be seen in Fig. 74 Despite the fact that other Irish factories employed other shapes the Edward's pre-dilection for the basic tapered shape lasted until the factory closed.

The Belfast decanters usually had two neck rings of the type illustrated in Fig. 76 bands of broad fluting frequently extending down the shoulder of the decanter from just below the bottom neck ring. Complemen-tary bands of narrower comb-fluting, whether mould-blown or wheel-cut, would extend upwards around the base, while the main body of the decanter would be mod-estly cut in curved festoons, simple incised pendants, and stars. More unusual forms of decoration were shallow scale flutes replac-ing the standard broad vertical fluting on the neck, and engraved festoons and floral motifs around the central body, in place of cutting.

Stoppers in tune with the pyriform body, usually took the form of flattened discs and later occasionally pear-shaped lozenges. The various styles are illustrated in Fig. 72, the general rule of thumb being that the earlier stoppers are the plainer ones, whereas after the turn of the nineteenth century decoration became more ornate.

Waterford

The famous glass-house at Waterford was built around 1783 by George and William Penrose who were rich Irish merchants. Its success and immediate reputation was established by bringing over the excellent workforce, headed by William Hill which was mentioned in the report to the Par-liamentary committee. Certainly its success meant that it continued in operation right up until 1851, long after the other factories had been forced to close down.

The traditional Waterford shape is that of the bulbous Prussian barrel-shape which was blown in two thicknesses, the thinner version for the lower end of the market, while the thicker, more elaborately cut ver-sions were aimed at those with money in their pockets. The base was usual decorated with moulded flutes, similar to the tradition

110

at Belfast, but the main body could also be decorated with a wide variety of motifs. In the early days these might take the form of a simple band of diamonds placed just below the shoulder, perhaps further embellished with decorative ornament between shoulder and lowest neck ring. But later the characteristic fine diamond began to make its appearance, completely enclosed in a shape outlined by mitre-cut lines. These areas of diamond cutting could either take the form of drapes from a single mitre line at the shoulder, or curved arches supported by squares of diamond cutting (Fig. 75).

The neck rings were almost always of the triple variety shown in Fig. 75, and usually there were three of them. The stopper though, is one of the keys to identifying Waterford decanters. It took the form of the traditional mushroom shape moulded in radial flutes, but the Waterford individuality was expressed in the additional ball of glass separating the mushroom head from the stopper shank.

Cork

The Cork Glass Company, which was founded in the same year as the Waterford

glass-house, had a much shorter life-span and closed in 1818. It also borrowed heavily from the shapes and designs of the other concerns. The general shape could be tapered or Prussian. It also employed either two or three neck rings according to mood, while stoppers could be mushroom, with or without a Waterford-style ball or disc-shaped like those on the Belfast decanters. The lower part of the body would be decorated with moulded flutes, while the cutters made extensive use of the fine interlacing diamond cut of the Waterford craftsmen.

So what are the distinguishing features of the Cork look? They lie in three main sections. Firstly the body shape. Although the Prussian and tapered styles were borrowed from Waterford and Belfast the neck was much longer and the shoulder much lower on the body than in other wares. Cork also added more shapes of their own, including the shouldered and cylindrical shapes. New innovations also came in the decoration of the neck rings (Fig. 76), but it was in the styles of cutting that the Cork craftsmen showed their true originality. The fine cut diamonds within mitred shapes may well have been borrowed from Waterloo, but the Cork artists also created a motif using only mitred curves which was peculiarly their own and is known to collectors as the

74

75

73

76

TRIANGULAR BELFAST

TRIPLE RING WATERFORD, CORK & WATERLOO

VERTICAL

FEATHERED

CORK

SQUARE

ROUNDED

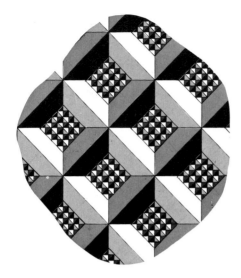 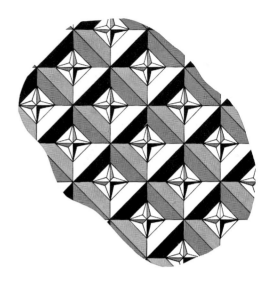

'Vesica' (Fig. 73). Basically, it consists of six, pointed ovals, linked together in a chain around the main body of the decanter. At the point where the ovals meet three radiating cuts are frequently found above and below the join, radiating in a fan shape, while the centre of the ovoid shape may feature a single eight-pointed star, be filled with cross-hatch diamonds, or a variety of other motifs. It is this vesica motif which is most closely associated with the Cork factory, and one much sought after by collectors.

Waterloo

The final major factory to be considered is that of the Waterloo Glass Company formed in 1815, much later than the other glass-houses, by Daniel Foley in Cork, remaining in operation until 1833. It obviously took its inspiration from Waterford using the same three triple neck rings, mushroom stopper, with or without the ball shank, and even loaned the vesica pattern from Cork. Its own individuality, however, was expressed in looped motifs linked with stylized bows, or in circular motifs.

These, then, were the classic early shapes and styles of the major Irish glass-houses throughout their production. But they were by no means the only variety on the market. As time passed the glass-makers in Ireland began to realize that in the absence of any glass taxes they could blow thicker decanters, and so use much deeper incisions to form the decoration. Gradually, they began to abandon the flimsier shouldered and tapered decanters, concentrating instead on the classic barrel-shaped Prussians, with its mushroom stopper, broad fluting to the shoulder, comb-fluting to the base and three neck rings. First, about the turn of the century, came the fashion for decorating the shoulder of the decanter in a geometric pattern of relief diamonds. With the passage of time this form of cutting gradually spread to include faceting on the neck rings. The basic rule of thumb is that the greater the area of cutting the later the period of the decanter. For a short while there was an interval when the body of the decanter would be divided either vertically or horizontally by deeply-cut mitred grooves into areas of differently-styled cutting. Two of the more popular favourites were the hobnail and the strawberry diamond (Fig. 77), but for further details of types of cut I recommend E M Elville's book *English and Irish Cut Glass* (1953).

Then came the gradual abolition of the neck rings. At first these were replaced by bands of step cutting, but gradually this extended to cover the whole of the neck area to the shoulder. Finally, the whole of the body might be covered in one type of cutting.

Before leaving the subject of Irish glass, one final point needs to be made. In the wake of the migrating English glass-blowers had come free-lance cutters and engravers who, if they would not find permanent work in the factories, would frequently set up in business on their own buying the plain blank decanters from the factories and then ornamenting them in their own individual style. Marsden Haddock of Cork 'supplies Cork and Waterford glass does the cutting himself, and also employs a cutter from England' is typical of the type of advertisement which these small-time cutters were putting in the daily newspapers of the day. This can confuse a collector who expects all decanters to comply with the basic mainstream shapes and styles which Westropp describes in full detail, but after a while one can hazard guesses as to which factory the blank decanter could be attributed. The Irish certainly dominated the first part of the Anglo-Irish period but by the end of the eighteenth century, the ten Irish glass-houses were incapable of meeting the seemingly insatiable world demand. Despite the ever increasing glass taxes, the English industry, with the arrival of mechanization in the early years of the nineteenth century, was able to double their output while still retaining the same workforce and so corner a large slice of the market.

Industrialization

Charles Chasbie of Stourbridge was the first to launch the glass industry into this

78 *A pair of Cork decanters, bearing the Cork Glass Company mark on the base which fetched £160 for the pair, despite the fact that one was slightly damaged, at the London salesroom of auctioneers W. and F.C. Bonham and Sons Ltd.*

new era of industrialization. He discovered a means of blowing shouldered vessels in an open and shut mould which, as new modifications flooded in, could be imprinted with the outline of the pattern in which the vessel was to be cut. This eliminated the painfully slow process of the cutter having to mark out his pattern on the decanter before commencing cutting.

Then in 1807 at a glass-house in Brettle Lane, Stourbridge, steam was first used to

79 *The later period of Anglo-Irish decanters: those on the top row are decorated with step cutting on the shoulder and neck.*

drive the cutting wheel. From now on decanters could have the rough pontil mark on the base ground smooth with little extra cost but, more important, the length of time it took to do the actual cutting was considerably reduced.

The benefits, however, were two-edged. Speed might be increased, but the old standards began to gradually wane. New establishments began to mushroom up throughout the country. The old small workforce of dedicated master-cutters was completely inadequate to meet the demands of this ever-expanding market. The business had to recruit more and more novices who had never held a cutting wheel in their lives before. Quality gradually lost out to quantity and during the first half of the nineteenth century, the cut-glass decanter gradually become more and more ornate until shape and form were completely submerged in an ocean of cut patterns and motifs.

The new shapes and new cuts

The favourite shapes for the Irish had been the Prussian and the taper. In addition to producing these shapes, England had also introduced the straight-sided cylinder between 1790 and the turn of the century. At first decoration was kept to a minimum, but the hand of the glass-cutter was soon at work. Around 1805 the shoulder of the cylinder usually sported a band of diamond cutting, with the body chamfered slightly, while the stopper might take on a faceted ball shape. Finally, around 1830 an earlier minor fashion for pillar-reeding came back into fashion, the whole of the lower part of the cylindrical body, from shoulder to base, being cut with deep vertical grooves the outer points of which would then be polished down to create a series of rounded pillars. The most popular cylindrical shape was that in which the shaped foot rim reappeared for the first time since Ravenscroft's decanter jugs. Along with the new cylindrical and square shapes came a new range of cut motifs.

One of the earliest designs had been that of the relief diamond which cut so deeply into the glass that only the tip of the diamond gave the outline of the original decanter form. Then around 1815 came the cross-cut diamond and the arrival of the highly popular strawberry diamond. The strawberry diamond frequently occurred in arched or rectangular vertical panels of decoration, and finally, around 1820, the cross-mitred hobnail pattern appeared.

The close of the eighteenth century had witnessed a uniformity of shape in the various styles of decanter. In the first quarter of the nineteenth century a much greater diversity began to creep in. By the 1820s the neck rings of the earlier Prussian shape were gradually becoming less pronounced and the emphasis on horizontal bands of cutting was giving way to a taste for the vertical. There are only three definite named shapes to be found at the end of the Regency period, the 'Royal', the 'Nelson' and the 'Fancy' which relied heavily on broad bands of faceting or fluting. It was a popular form which spread right across the Continent at the height of the European Empire style and even found its way on to the tables of the Royal House of Russia.

From the 1830s onwards the taste for lavish cut-decoration gradually waned only to be briefly revitalized in 1845 when the Glass Excise Act was repealed, and the industry again plunged into an orgy of deep-cut mitre work on much thicker and heavier glass, this time with curvilinear motifs rather than the rigidly vertical or horizontal. But the public was beginning to suffer from indigestion after being fed so much rich ornamentation. A reaction began to set in, and once the peak had been reached in the glassware at the Great Exhibition of 1851, cut glass fell totally from favour in England.

European imitations – especially France

Throughout the 1780 to 1830 period, the rapid expansion of the Anglo-Irish glass industry had been enviously watched by glass-makers elsewhere in Europe. The Swedes, for example, found that their locally produced engraved glass was being eclipsed by the Anglo-Irish cut-style. The art of cutting which had been first introduced in the 1730s had to be revived, and by the 1830s and 40s the Kungsholm and Kosta works were in full production of Prussian decanters, complete with faceted neck-rings and mushroom-stopper, the cutting that of the early Anglo-Irish period, plain and uncluttered.

In France, the success of the English crystal glass had a slightly different effect. During the early part of the nineteenth century a strict customs-barrier was maintained against imported glass, and a conscious effort was made to encourage the home industry to experiment in the field of decorative tablewares. As early as 1782 the Cristalleries de Saint-Louis had begun production of the English lead crystal metal, but it was to be at Baccarat that France's greatest cut-glass was to be produced. Protected by restriction on Anglo-Irish wares, the Baccarat glass-cutters could draw their inspiration from across the Channel, but rather than being content to purely imitate they soon developed a distinctive Empire style of their own. Where the English motifs were composed of ever more complicated designs of intersecting straight-mitred grooves the French developed a taste for the technically more difficult curved-cutting. To achieve any sort of cut the decanter had to be held above the wheel and lowered onto it for the incision to be made. The glass-cutter was therefore working 'blind' in that he could not see the cut as it was being made. Of the two types the straight-cut was by far the easiest the cutter guiding the decanter in a straight line and judging the appropriate time to lift the decanter away from the wheel to leave a line of the correct length. Curved cutting on the other hand, required much greater skill. To decorate a decanter or jug with a series of Empire drapes the cutter had to judge, with absolute accuracy, both the depth of the curve and its precise beginning and end. The curved cut was shown to its best advantage on the French equivalent of the Georgian claret decanter (TYPE 19b), with the body bulbous as opposed to the Anglo-Irish cylindrical. Another alternative, at Baccarat, was the style of Prussian decanter (TYPE 18p), the body, blown of more cylindrical contour was cut in deep rounded pillar-fluting, a unique Baccarat feature being an inset circle of glass covering an enamelled heraldic device.

At the Saint-Louis factory the neo-classical style was expressed in an early semi-fluted version of the urn-shaped decanter (TYPE 19j), frequently further ornamented with restrained gilding and accompanied by a matching set of glasses in the same mode of decoration.

Keynote to all French production was a simple elegance of cut which refrained from the excesses of ornamentation in which the early nineteenth-century English and Irish industries indulged.

American imitations

In America, it was the firm of Messrs Bakewell, Page and Bakewell in Pittsburgh, who first began to produce fine quality cut glass. The firm was founded in 1807 by two Englishmen, Benjamin Bakewell and Edward Ensell, who ensured that the first employees included a highly-skilled nucleus of English and Irish cutters. Until the

---

80 An excellent example of the high quality cut-glass ware produced by Bakewell, Page and Bakewell at their Pittsburgh Flint Glass Works, c. 1825. (Corning Museum of Glass, Corning, New York).

116

81 A blown decanter engraved with a floral pattern and the inscription 'John H. Leighton' made by the New England Glass Company, Cambridge Massachusetts c. 1850–1855. (Corning Museum of Glass, Corning, New York.)

advent of Bakewell's none of the American glass-houses had attempted cutting on any large scale. Most of the larger firms were on the east coast where there was too much Anglo-Irish glassware flooding the market for the local industry to compete. In Pittsburgh, however, the situation was different. Cut off from reasonably cheap supplies of cut glass by the Allegheny Mountains it was natural that sooner or later the mid-West should produce its own cut glass.

Unlike other factories, where in the first few years of operation only bottle and window glass might be made, the Bakewell factory began producing cut and engraved glass from the first moment its doors opened in 1808. The gamble paid off and within only a short while the Bakewell reputation for highest quality table glass was well established. By 1817, President Monroe himself ordered a glass service from them. Another service found its way onto the table of Andrew Jackson when he was President, while General Lafayette, visiting the factory in 1824, readily affirmed that the Bakewell glass was equal in quality to that produced by the finest French factories of the day.

Their decanters followed closely on the fashions of the imported Anglo-Irish wares, of which the barrel-shape was the most popular. They introduced the hollow-blown ball stoppers, either plain or pattern moulded, at about the same time as the English industry, but they retained the neck rings long after they had fallen out of favour in England. Characteristic of the Bakewell decanters is the fact that cutting was never carried to the same excesses as in England or Ireland.

The decanter in Fig. 80 illustrates Bakewell's production at its best and explains why Deming Jarves later referred to Mr Bakewell as 'the father of the flint-glass business in this country'. It is only sparingly decorated around the base with strawberry diamond motifs, the fluting on the shoulder being kept to a minimum and the cut decoration on the stopper bold yet simple. In short, the overall proportions are excellent. Small wonder then, that, with decanters like these, the Bakewell Company managed to walk off with most of the top prizes at the exhibitions of glassware held at the Franklin Institute in Philadephia. To quote one of the proud locals in a letter of 1826: 'The glass of Pittsburgh and the parts adjacent, is known and sold from Maine to New Orleans. Even in Mexico they quaff the beverage from the beautiful white flint of Messrs Bakewell Page and Bakewell of our city.'

The New England Glass Company

While the Bakewell factory was the first to commercially produce cut glass on a large scale, it was not long before its success caught the attention of the industry in the East, the first major competitor being the New England Glass Company (N.E.G.C. for abbreviation) of Cambridge, Massachusetts. It opened its doors in 1817 and right up until the closing years of the nineteenth century maintained its high standards of cutting despite the popularity of pressed and mould-blown glass. Like Bakewell it followed the Anglo-Irish cutting traditions closely in the early years, preferring the lighter cuts to the deep brilliant cuts of the full Regency period. Of the many Irish factories it was the wares from Waterford which the New England Company seemed to favour most, always using their flawless lead-formula glass for these quality wares.

If anything the New England Glass Company's decanters show an even greater restraint than those of Bakewell & Co, especially during the mid-nineteenth century when the Victorian taste for over-ornamentation was at its peak elsewhere. The decanter in Fig. 81 is from this period. Made of heavy glass, the body is typically engraved in the New England fashion with lightly executed motifs of fruiting vine and wreaths of flowers.

By 1823, N.E.G.C.'s output was enormous, with some 22,400 pounds of glassware leaving the factory per week to be eagerly absorbed both in America and abroad. Obviously, in the face of such demand there was great potential for anyone who could produce a cheaper glass more quickly than by the laborious hand-cut method. The answer was mechanically produced glass.

Mechanization and innovators

In his treatise, 'The Principles of Glass-Making' written some sixty years later, the English glass expert Harry J Powell described the three basic methods of production. 'In the process of moulding glass, the molten mass is forced to take the form of the mould, both on its inner and outer surface, by the pressure of the glass-blower's breath' – this is known to collectors as 'contact mould glass'. 'In pressing glass, the molten glass takes the form of the mould upon its outer surface under the pressure of the metallic plunger, driven by mechanical means, while the inner surface is modelled by the plunger itself' – this is known to collectors as 'pressed glass'. 'For articles of greater complexity, the moulds are made in two or more divisions, hinged together, and opening outwards by means of two handles, to facilitate the delivery of the glass' – this is known to collectors as 'Blown Three-Mould'.

As in other specialist fields, experts frequently disagree among themselves; and the same is true of glass collectors, especially when it comes to the correct terminology for the various mechanical processes, but as far as this book is concerned the various types are referred to as 'patterned glass', in the hope that this does not offend those who are more technically minded.

The earliest form of modern, as opposed to ancient, pattern-moulding had been that employed by the English and Irish to create the bands of fluting at the base of their

decanters. Both Stiegel and Amelung had also used it and in the Mid-West it had been slightly adapted to form definite swirled, diamond and 'broken-rib' designs. In England, as early at 1802, Charles Chasbie of Stourbridge had developed the use of an open and shut mould which produced blanks with the outline of the cutting pattern already clearly visible upon it. But the English failed to recognize, as the Americans did, that this idea could be extended so that decanters could be blown complete with a design on which no further cutting would be necessary.

Both moulded and pressed versions of patterned glass began to appear on the American market in the 1820s. Over the next ten to fifteen years a whole flood of patents were granted for improvements to the basic processes. It was the blown-mould method which was first widely used in the making of decanters while the pressed-glass method was only applied to objects like plates and door-knobs until 1830 when a Pennsylvanian glass-maker was granted a patent for the manufacture of 'Glass, Bottles, Decanters of all Kinds, and other Pressed Hollow Glass ware, with the Necks Smaller than the Cavity or inside Diameter of the Vessel'. Certainly by 1845 nearly every home in America was using pressed glass plates, sugar bowls, milk jugs, cruets, and a whole range of other pressed glass ware.

Deming Jarves and blown-three-mould

The exact innovators of these processes are unknown, but the man who first saw the potential of their use on a grand scale was Deming Jarves who opened his Boston and Sandwich glass works on Independence Day in 1825. At first he relied on traditional blowing methods for making his hollow wares, two-ringed decanters being among the earliest of his recorded styles, but they were always much cruder than those produced at either Bakewell's or the New England Glass Company. As late as 1880 the rough pontil mark was still being left on the base of his decanters. Instead of trying to compete, he turned his attention to the new mechanical processes and under his direction the Sandwich Company was to become one of the largest producers of Blown Three Mould patterned glass, in both clear and coloured metal. Jarves' first patent was granted in 1828, the year in which he was joined in the company by another highly inventive glass-maker Hiram Dillaway. Using a high-quality metal, of lead or barium, his decanters soon closely resembled the cut-glass wares of the Anglo-Irish period.

The market which Jarves had started was soon to become highly competitive. John and Thomas Bakewell, having patented a mechanical method of producing blown glass in the mould, had soon entered the race. So too had the N.E.G.C. who had made the first pressed glass article in 1827. The industry was continually bombarded by new short-cuts to production, but the next major breakthrough came in 1864 when William Leighton, once an employee at N.E.G.C., patented his new *soda-lime formula* for glass. The expensive ingredient in high-quality glass had always been the lead content. Under Leighton's new formula this was omitted and cheaper lime substituted. The price dropped accordingly and the new soda-lime glass was as much as half the price of the expensive flint glass. The new lime glass might not have had the same brilliance as lead glass, or been as easily cut and engraved, but it was an ideal medium for the new mechanically produced patterned glass. With an even cheaper product on their hands the American glass companies embarked on such an era of expansion as had never been seen

---

82 A blown three mould decanter in yellow-olive green glass, decorated in the geometric pattern C11-6 with a green waffled disc stopper. Possibly from the glassworks of Park, Edmonds and Park, Kent, Ohio, c. 1823–30. (Corning Museum of Glass, Corning, New York).

83 An American clear glass decanter with blown mould decoration c. 1835 (Victoria and Albert Museum).

before. In the early days, the aim had been to duplicate the fancy cuts of the Anglo-Irish period, but, from the 1840s onwards, the American industry began to develop its own highly individual styles of decoration which were more suited to both the medium and the mechanical processes which they were using. It was not long before companies were coming up with some new pattern or design in virtually every week of production.

Typical of the early period is the blown-three-mould decanter in Fig. 82 which dates from around 1823 to 1830 and was possibly made at the glass-works of Park, Edmonds and Park of Kent, Ohio. The overall shape is very similar to the English shouldered decanters of a slightly earlier period, while the splitting up of the decoration into vertical areas of geometric-pattern flutes and diamonds is typical of the Anglo-Irish style of the day. Similarly the later decanter in Fig. 83 which dates from around 1835 and shows the phase for arched cut decoration which was so popular about the same period in England. In both cases the softness of line shows that the pieces come from the early days of patterned glass when the moulds had still not been sufficiently developed to completely mimic the sharp edges of the true cut glass. Compare these with the Sandwich decanter in Fig. 86 which typifies the beginnings of a move away from the imported styles towards a greater boldness of pattern. The star may well have been a popular decanter motif in England, but it was always accompanied by other areas of deep cutting. In the hands of the Sandwich designers the star has become the focal point of both stopper and body, the remaining area being filled in with bold curved fluting. Fig. 87 shows the new designs taken one step further in the form of the 'Sandwich chain pattern', a much bolder decoration the like of which was unknown in cut-glass wares.

The main reason for the development of completely new and uniquely American motifs was the fact that, as yet, the mould

122

*84 Ornate gilding married to the brilliance of
blue produce classic Bieidermeier opulence.*

85 *Popular patterns such as the 'Horn of Plenty' illustrated here were reproduced in large quantities. (Corning Museum of Glass, Corning, New York).*

process did not produce the crisp mitred outlines which was the hallmark of true Anglo-Irish glass. Nevertheless, once mechanical processes began to improve the manufacturers soon reverted to the 'cut' look, marrying it with the bolder, uniquely American motifs. Fig. 88 is an excellent example of this 'marriage', the shoulder, neck and stopper showing typical cut motifs while the squirls and circles on the body echo early blown-mould patterned glass.

The final stage of development (Fig. 89), from the 1860s onwards, was for the decanter to be ensuite with a whole range of similarly patterned tableware from glasses and tumblers, to cruet sets and jugs, made with the classic, sharp-edged cut-look. Commercially successful and popular patterns would be named (the decanter in Fig. 90 for example, being made in the New England Glass Company's 'Honeycomb' pattern), but this did not protect makers from pirating. Soon the pressure to keep turning out more and more novelty patterns was so great that few of the glasshouses took either time or trouble to patent their patterns. So it is that patterns like the 'Horn of Plenty' (Fig. 85) were reproduced in vast quantities by more than one factory.

The range of American patterned glass is immense and often confusing, but fortunately those who want to make a specialized collection of pressed or moulded decanters there are three essential books on the subject: *Blown Moulded Glass* and *Sandwich Glass*, both by Ruth Webb Lee and *American Pressed Glass and Figure Bottles* by Albert Christian Revi.

When the Americans exhibited their new patterned glass at Crystal Palace in 1851 the British reaction is best summed up by a quote from the *Illustrated Encyclopaedia of the Great Exhibition* in London, 'by pressing into moulds this elegant material is produced to the public at prices considerably lower than those at which cut flint glass could be possibly offered. Many of the specimens of pressed glass exhibited have a degree of sharpness in all ornamental parts

which renders it difficult, without a close examination, to say whether or not they have been subjected to the glass-cutter's wheel'.

It could have spelt disaster for the English master-cutters, who could not possibly create hand-made cut glass as economically as the Americans with their mass-production. However, at the same Great Exhibition there appeared the new coloured Bohemian glass in the Biedermeier style which was to keep the English, American and European glass-cutters fully occupied over the next twenty years.

As explained in the previous chapter, the earliest nineteenth-century Bohemian decanters took the form of clear cased or flashed glass engraved through colour to colourless. This was followed by a far more ornate version, around the 1830s and 1840s, which involved the use of the cutting wheel.

In the fancier cut-glass of this Biedermeier period the body of the decanter would be blown from translucent red or blue coloured glass and then cased with milky-white opaque glass. Occasionally, further layers of coloured glass would be added before the final opaque casing to give an even more opulent look. The cutter then applied his wheel to the outer opaque casing to reveal contrasting areas of coloured glass beneath the outer surface. It was a style quickly imitated by the rest of Europe and America. Frequently the cuts took the form of gothic arches on the neck, while the body would be but with a series of 'printies' or shallow circular cuts (TYPE 19e). To gild the lily even more the opaque areas might be further ornamented with hand-painting in the style of the porcelain decoration of the day. Indeed of the main exhibits at the stand of George Bacchus & Sons at the Great Exhibition of 1851 there was just such a ruby and white enamel cased decanter, engraved and delicately overpainted.

Another unusually fine example is the ruby and opaque decanter in Fig. 91 made by the Birmingham manufacturers George Bacchus & Co, and exhibited by them at the Exhibition of Modern British Manufacturers at the Royal Society of Arts in 1850. It is unusual in that the cutting takes the form of

diamonds, the base and the top of the stopper being decorated with the familiar star cut of the Anglo-Irish period.

The arrival of the new 'brilliant' cut

As the taste for the Bohemian cased and coloured glass faded in the 1860s and 1870s it was replaced by a new vogue for American cut crystal glass. New deposits of sand had been found in the Mid-West which lead to a much clearer metal. Known to collectors as the 'brilliant' period, it was an era of great ornamentation with complicated and elaborate cutting covering every inch of the vessels.

The new brilliant cut made its appearance at the 1876 Centennial Exposition in Philadelphia, and such was its success that it was to be a dominant style for the next forty years, names to lead the field including the Libbey Glass Company (an offshoot of N.E.G.C.), T.G. Hawkes, O. Dorflinger & Sons, the Mount Washington Glass Company, and Hobbs, Brockunier Company.

By the late 1880s the vogue had spread to Europe with T.G. Hawkes carrying off the Grand Prize at the 1889 Paris Exposition for their Grecian-style cut-glass. The new style of cutting involved decorating wares with as many as five or six different types of interlocking cut. Colourless glass showed off the brilliance of the cuts to best advantage, but many of the leading companies also experimented with cutting to colourless through transparent cranberry, blue, green, ruby, amethyst or amber.

The complexity of the patterns and the minute detail with which they were executed meant that brilliant glass was

91 A ruby and opaque white-glazed decanter diamond cut by George Bacchus and Sons Birmingham, c. 1864. (Victoria and Albert Museum).

92 *Throughout the second half of the nineteenth-century, when hand-cut glass was becoming rare there was always keen demand for really top quality pieces. These two silver-mounted claret jugs typify the craftsmanship still surviving through the years of falling demand.*

extremely expensive. Inevitably, the less scrupulous companies began to find ways of speeding up the painstakingly slow hand-cut method. In the early days each piece had been an individual one, the cutter combining various motifs according to his own whim, but soon standard patterns began to appear and cutters were provided with moulded blanks already imprinted with the pressed cut pattern which could be finished off by hand to give it an 'expensive hand-made look'. The next step was open mass-production of the same cut glass patterns. Just as the Americans fifty years earlier had put an end to the English cut-glass era by flooding the market with patterned glass reproductions in the Anglo-Irish style, so they put an end to their own cut-glass market with their own mass-production of the 'brilliant' cut.

By the dawn of the twentieth century, heavily cut 'brilliant' glass was falling into disrepute. In its place the companies producing quality cut wares were using bolder floral motifs similar to the shallow highly polished engraving carried out by the Bohemian craftsmen over two centuries before. The wheel had come full circle.

Acknowledgements

Bonham and Sons Ltd. 113; Central Museum and Art Gallery, Northampton 36; Christie Manson and Wood 65, 79, 94 (*above*), 102; Corning Museum of Glass, Corning, New York 60, 91 (*right*), 92 (*below*), 101 (*below*), 116, 118, 120–121, 124; Cooper Bridgeman Library 18; Delomosne and Sons 74, 88, 89, 114; Dudley Art Gallery 35, 38, 58; London Museum 18; Phillip Son and Neale 39, 77; Pilkington Glass Museum 18; Sotheby King and Chasemore 61 (*above*); Sotheby Parke Bernet, London 71, 72, 75, 84, 85, 90; Victoria and Albert Museum, London 7, 9, 10, 11, 12, 13, 14, 16, 18, 20, 23, 31, 56, 59, 61 (*below*), 62, 63, 64, 66, 70, 73, 74, 76, 80 (*both*), 82, 83, 87, 90–91, 93, 96, 98, 100 (*top*), 108, 122, 126; Paul Willatts 7, 10, 14, 23, 30, 59, 70, 74, 82, 127.

While every effort has been made to correctly credit sources, apologies are made for any omissions.

X